C000261309

CHESHIRE

A GENEALOGICAL BIBLIOGRAPHY

Volume 1

Cheshire Genealogical Sources

by

Stuart A. Raymond

Published by the
Federation of Family History Societies (Publications) Ltd,
The Benson Room, Birmingham & Midland Institute,
Margaret Street, Birmingham, B3 3BS, England

Copies also obtainable from:

S.A. & M.J. Raymond, 6, Russet Avenue, Exeter, EX1 3QB, U.K.

First Published 1995

Cataloguing in publication data:

Raymond, Stuart A., 1945-
Cheshire: a genealogical bibliography. 2 vols British genealogical
bibliographies. Birmingham, England: Federation of Family History
Societies, 1995. Vol. 1. Cheshire genealogical sources. Vol. 2. Cheshire
family histories and pedigrees.

DDC 016.9291094271

ISBN 1-86006-011-0

ISSN 1033-2065

Contents

VOLUME 1: Cheshire Genealogical Sources

VOLUME 2: Cheshire Family Histories and Pedigrees

Introduction

This bibliography is intended primarily for genealogists. It is, however, hoped that it will also prove useful to historians, librarians, archivists, research students, and anyone else interested in the history of Cheshire. Both volumes of this work are intended to be used in conjunction with my *English genealogy: an introductory bibliography,* and the other volumes in the *British genealogical bibliographies* series. A full list of these volumes appears on the back cover. The area covered is the historic county of Cheshire, as it existed prior to local government reorganisation in 1974. This volume is devoted primarily to works on genealogical source material; volume two lists published family histories and pedigrees, biographical dictionaries and heraldry.

Many genealogists, when they begin their research, do not realise just how much information has been published, and is readily available in printed form. Not infrequently, they head straight for the archives, rather than checking printed sources first. In so doing, they waste much time, and also impose needless wear and tear on irreplaceable archives. However, when faced with the vast array of tomes possessed by major reference libraries, it is difficult to know where to begin without guidance. This bibliography is intended to point you in the right direction. My aim has been to list everything relating to Cheshire that has been published and is likely to be of use to genealogists. In general, I have not included works which are national in scope but which have local content. Many such works may be identified in *English genealogy: an introductory bibliography,* to which reference is made at appropriate points below. I have also excluded the numerous notes and queries found in family history society and similar journals, except where the content is of importance. Where I have included such notes, replies to them are cited in the form 'see also', with no reference to the names of respondents. Local and church histories have been excluded except in a few cases. They frequently provide invaluable information for the genealogist, but are far too numerous to be listed here. This is a bibliography of published works; hence the many manuscript histories, transcripts, *etc.,* to be found in Cheshire libraries are excluded.

Be warned: just because information has been published, it does not necessarily follow that it is accurate. I have not made any judgement on the accuracy of most works listed: that is up to you. If you are able, it is always best to check printed sources against their originals, to determine how accurate the editor was.

Anyone who tries to compile a totally comprehensive bibliography of Cheshire is likely to fall short of his aim. The task is almost impossible, especially if the endeavour is made by one person. That does not, however, mean that the attempt should not be made. Usefulness, rather than comprehensiveness, has been my prime aim - and this book will not be useful to anyone if its publication were to be prevented by a vain attempt to ensure total comprehensiveness. I am well aware that there are likely to be omissions - although none, I hope, of books which every Cheshire genealogist should examine. My purpose has been to enable you to identify works which are mostly readily available, and which can be borrowed via the inter-library loan network irrespective of whether you live in London or Melbourne. Most public libraries are able to tap into this network; your local library should be able to borrow most items I have listed, even if it has to go overseas to obtain them.

If you are an assiduous researcher, you may well come across items I have missed. If you do, please let me know, so that they can be included in the next edition.

The work of compiling this bibliography has depended heavily on the resources of the libraries I have used. These included Cheshire Record Office, Stockport Local Heritage Library, Chester City Record Office, Chester Public Library, Manchester Public Library, Exeter University Library, Exeter City Library, the British Library, and the Society of Genealogists, amongst others. I am grateful to the librarians of all these institutions for their help. I am grateful too for the assistance rendered by the three family history societies in Cheshire, and particularly to Peter Dewdney and Brenda Smith. Brian Christmas and Brett Langston both kindly read and commented on early drafts of the book, Jean Smith typed the manuscript, and Bob Boyd saw the book through the press. I am grateful too to the officers of the Federation of Family History Societies, whose support is vital for the continuation of this series. My thanks also to my wife Marjorie, and to Paul and Mary, who have lived with this book for many months.

Stuart A. Raymond

Libraries and Record Offices

Chester Library,
Northgate Street,
CHESTER,
Cheshire,
CH1 2EF

Stockport Local Heritage Library,
Stockport Central Library,
Wellington Road South,
STOCKPORT,
SK1 3RS

Cheshire Record Office,
Duke Street,
Chester,
Cheshire,
CH1 1RL

Chester City Record Office,
Town Hall,
Chester,
Cheshire,
CH1 2HJ

John Rylands University Library of Manchester,
Oxford Road,
Manchester,
M13 9PP

In addition, most public libraries have local collections relating to their own localities. For full details, see the *Directory of local studies in North West England,* cited below, section 2.

Abbreviations

A.N.Q.	*Advertiser notes and queries*
C.F.H.	*Cheshire family historian*
C.N.Q.	*Cheshire notes and queries*
C.P.R.M.	*Cheshire parish registers: marriages*
C.Sf.	*Cheshire sheaf*
Cm.S.	Chetham Society
F.H.S.C.	Family History Society of Cheshire
F.H.S.C.J.	*Family History Society of Cheshire Journal*
H.S.L.C.	*Transactions of the Historic Society of Lancashire and Cheshire*
J.C.A.H.S.	*Journal of the Chester Archaeological and Historic Society*
J.L.D.L.H.S.	*Journal of the Lymm and District Local History Society*
L.C.A.S.	*Transactions of the Lancashire and Cheshire Antiquarian Society*
L.C.R.S.	Lancashire and Cheshire Record Society
L.G.	*Local Gleanings*
M.G.H.	*Miscellanea genealogica et heraldica*
N.C.F.H.	*North Cheshire family historian*
N.C.F.H.S.	North Cheshire Family History Society
N.S.	New series
O.S.	Old series
P.N.	*Palatine note-book*
P.P.R.S.	Phillimore's parish register series
Q.J.L.D.	*Quarterly journal of the Lymm and District Local History Society*

Bibliographic Presentation

Authors' names are in SMALL CAPITALS. Book and journal titles are in *italics*. Articles appearing in journals, and material such as parish register transcripts, forming only part of books are in inverted commas and textface type. Volume numbers are in **bold** and the individual number of the journal may be shown in parentheses. These are normally followed by the place of publication (except where this is London, which is omitted), the name of the publisher and the date of publication. In the case of articles, further figures indicate page numbers.

1. THE HISTORY OF CHESHIRE

In order to reach an understanding of our ancestors' lives, it is necessary to study the society in which they lived. This will also enable us to appreciate the conditions which gave rise to parish registers, census returns and the many other sources the genealogist needs to consult. Much has been written on the history of Cheshire, and a comprehensive listing cannot be given in this section. The works cited below are either authoritative in their field, use sources of interest to genealogists for wider historical purposes, or contain useful genealogical information. The authoritative, but incomplete, work on the history of the county is:

HARRIS, B.E. *A history of the County of Chester.* Victoria county history series. 3 vols to date. Oxford University Press for the Institute of Historical Research, 1979. Contents: v.1. includes Domesday book. v.2. Administrative history, Parliamentary representation. v.3. Ecclesiastical and educational history.

Other useful county-wide studies include:

FREEMAN, T.W., RODGERS, H.B., & KINVIG, R.H. *Lancashire, Cheshire and the Isle of Man.* Nelson, 1966. Historical geography.

PEVSNER, NIKOLAUS & HUBBARD, EDWARD. *Cheshire.* Buildings of England. Penguin Books, 1971.

ASHMORE, OWEN. *The industrial archaeology of North-West England.* Cm.S., 3rd series **29**. 1982. Gazetteer covering both Lancashire and Cheshire.

Historians of the nineteenth century and earlier provided much more information of genealogical relevance than is usual in later writers, frequently including monumental inscriptions, pedigrees, extracts from parish registers, *etc.* Some of the earlier histories are essentially surveys of parochial history, which trace descents of manors, list clergy, print monumental inscriptions, and provide much other local information. The following list of early works is arranged by date:

KING, DANIEL. *The Vale-Royall of England, or, the County Palatine of Chester ...* Daniel King, 1656. Reprinted in *The printed sources of Western Art* series, **20**. Portland, Oregon: Collegium Graphicum, 1972. Also reprinted in Ormerod, see below. The earliest history of

the county; includes list of the gentry and various officials, a few monumental inscriptions, *etc.*

I[RVINE], W.F., [ed] 'Randle Holmes's survey of Cheshire, 1668 [1671]', *C.Sf.* 3rd series **45-7** & **49**, 1951-6, *passim.* Extracts from an early, otherwise unpublished, survey of Cheshire manors.

LEYCESTER, SIR PETER. *Some antiquities touching Cheshire, faithfully collected out of authentique histories, old deeds, records and evidences.* [ ], 1672. Reprinted in Ormerod, see below. Parochial survey, giving many descents of manors, *etc.*

GASTRELL, FRANCIS. *Notitia Cestriensis, or historical notices of the Diocese of Chester.* Cm. S., O.S. **8**, 1845. vol. 1. Cheshire. A parochial survey, including many inscriptions; early 18th c.

[GOWER, F.] *A sketch of the materials for a new history of Cheshire,* ed. W.Latham. 3rd ed. G. & W.Nicol, 1800. Includes list of source material.

BARLOW, T.WORTHINGTON. *Cheshire: its historical and literary associations, illustrated in a series of biographical sketches.* Manchester: Bell, 1855.

ORMEROD, GEORGE. *The history of the County Palatine and City of Chester, compiled from original evidences in public offices, the Harleian and Cottonian mss., parochial registers, private muniments, unpublished ms. collections of successive Cheshire antiquaries, and a personal survey of every township in the county, incorporated with a republication of King's Vale Royal and Leycester's Cheshire antiquities.* 3 vols. 2nd ed., revised by Thomas Helsby. George Routledge and Sons, 1882. Vol.3, covering the Hundred of Macclesfield, reprinted Manchester: E.J. Morten, 1980. The standard parochial survey, including manorial descents, pedigrees, lists of clergy, memorial inscriptions, *etc., etc.*

Three works provide parochial surveys of particular hundreds:

EARWAKER, J.P. *East Cheshire past and present, or a history of the Hundred of Macclesfield in the County Palatine of Chester, from original records.* 2 vols. The author, 1877-80. Includes many pedigrees, monumental inscriptions, and extracts from original sources.

MORTIMER, WILLIAM WILLIAMS. *The history of the Hundred of Wirral, with a sketch of the City and County of Chester, compiled from the earliest authentic records.* Whittaker & Co., 1847. Reprinted Manchester: E.J. Marten, 1972.

SULLEY, PHILIP. *The Hundred of Wirrall.* Birkenhead: B.Haram and Co., 1889. Includes monumental inscriptions, notes on descents, etc.

Most modern works on Cheshire history deal with particular periods. The following list is arranged in rough chronological order.

HUSAIN, B.M.C. *Cheshire under the Norman Earls, 1066-1237.* History of Cheshire 4. Chester: Cheshire Community Council, 1973.

TAIT, JAMES. 'Knight service in Cheshire', *English historical review* 57, 1942, 437-59. 12-13th c., general study.

MORGAN, PHILIP. *War and society in mediaeval Cheshire, 1277-1403.* Cm.S., 3rd series 34. 1987. Includes bibliography.

HEWITT, H.J. *Cheshire under the three Edwards.* A history of Cheshire, 5. Chester: Cheshire Community Council, 1967.

HEWITT, H.J. *Mediaeval Cheshire: an economic and social history of Cheshire in the reigns of the three Edwards.* Cm.S., N.S. 88. 1929.

BENNETT, MICHAEL J. *Community, class and careerism: Cheshire and Lancashire society in the age of Sir Gawain and the Green Knight.* Cambridge: Cambridge University Press, 1983.

BENNETT, MICHAEL. 'Sir Gawain and the Green Knight and the literary, achievement of the north-west Midlands: the historical background', *Journal of medieval history* 5, 1879, 63-89. Discussion of Cheshire society, late 14th. c.

BOOTH, P.H.W. 'Taxation and public order: Cheshire in 1353', *Northern history* 12, 1976, 16-31.

McNIVEN, P. 'The Cheshire Rising of 1400', *Bulletin of the John Rylands Library* 52, 1969-70, 375-96.

DRIVER, J.T. *Cheshire in the later middle ages, 1399-1540.* A history of Cheshire 6. Chester: Cheshire Community Council, 1971.

BENNETT, MICHAEL J. 'Sources and problems in the study of social mobility: Cheshire in the later middle ages,' *H.S.L.C.* 128, 1979, 59-95.

MORRIS, RUPERT, H. *Chester in the Plantagenet and Tudor reigns.* Chester: the author, [1893]. Includes many extracts from the muniments of Chester.

BECK, JOAN. *Tudor Cheshire.* A history of Cheshire. 7. Chester: Cheshire Community Council, 1969.

GROVES, JILL. *Piggins, husslements and desperate debts: a social history of North-East Cheshire through wills and probate inventories, 1600-1760.* Between the Bollin and the Mersey series 1. Sale: Northern Writers Advisory Service. 1994. Analysis of c. 500 probate documents from Altrincham, Ashton upon Mersey, Baguley, Bowdon, Dunham Massey, Gatley, Hale, Northenden, Sale, Timperley, and Wythenshaw. Edited transcripts of probate records for these parishes are to appear in future volumes of the series.

HIGGINS, G.P. 'The government of early Stuart Cheshire,' *Northern history* 12, 1976, 32-52.

HAIGH, C.A. 'Slander and the church courts in the sixteenth century,' *L.C.A.S.* 78, 1975, 1-13. Based on records of the Consistory Court of the Bishop of Chester.

THORNTON, T. 'The integration of Cheshire into the Tudor nation state in the early sixteenth century,' *Northern history* 29, 1993, 40-63.

HAIGH, C.A. 'Finance and administration in a new diocese: Chester, 1541-1641,' in O'DAY, ROSEMARY & HEAL, FELICITY, eds. *Continuity and change: personnel and administration of the church in England, 1500-1642.* Leicester: Leicester University Press, 1876, 145-66

CURTIS, T.C. 'Quarter sessions appearances and their background: a seventeenth-century regional study,' in COCKBURN, J.S., ed. *Crime in England 1550-1800.* Methuen, 1977, 135-54. Based on Cheshire Quarter Sessions records.

RICHARDSON, R.C. *Puritanism in North-West England: a regional study of the Diocese of Chester to 1642.* Manchester: Manchester University Press, 1972.

MANNING, R.B. 'The making of a Protestant aristocracy; the ecclesiastical commissioners of the Diocese of Chester 1550-98', *Bulletin of the Institute of Historical Research* 49, 1976, 60-79.

ADDY, JOHN. *Sin and society in the seventeenth century.* Routledge, 1989. Based on cause papers in the Chester Diocesan records.

MORRILL, J.S. *Cheshire, 1630-1660: County government and society during the English Revolution.* Oxford University Press, 1974.

LAKE, P. 'The collection of ship money in Cheshire during the sixteen thirties: a case study of relations between central and local government', *Northern history* 17, 1981, 44-71.

MARCOTTE, E. 'Shrieval administration of Ship Money in Cheshire 1637: limitations of early Stuart governance', *Bulletin of the John Rylands Library* 58, 1975-76, 137-72.

DORE, R.N. *The Civil Wars in Cheshire.* A History of Cheshire 8. Chester: Cheshire Community Council, 1966.

JOHNSON, A.M. Politics in Chester during the Civil Wars and Interregnum', in CLARK, PETER & SLACK, PAUL, eds. *Crisis and order in English towns, 1500-1700.* Routledge & Kegan Paul, 1972, 204-36.

MALBON, THOMAS. *Memorials of the Civil War in Cheshire and the adjacent counties ...,* ed. James Hall. L.C.R.S., 19. 1889. Includes a list of soldiers buried at Nantwich, 1643-6, from the parish register.

MORRILL, JOHN. 'The allegiance of the Cheshire gentry in the Great Civil War', *L.C.A.S.* 77. 1967, 47-76. Includes a note on sources.

PINCKNEY, PAUL J. 'The Cheshire elections of 1656', *Bulletin of the John Rylands Library* 49, 1967, 387-426

JONES, J.R. 'Booth's rising of 1659', *Bulletin of the John Rylands Library* 39, 1956-7, 416-43.

HODDON, HOWARD. *Cheshire 1660-1780: Restoration to Industrial Revolution.* History of Cheshire 9. Chester: Cheshire Community Council, 1978.

CHALLINOR, P.J. 'Restoration and exclusion in the County of Chester', *Bulletin of the John Ryland Library* 64, 1981-2, 360-85.

BURNE, R.V.H. 'The treatment of the poor in the eighteenth century in Cheshire', *J.C.A.H.S.* 52, 1965, 33-48.

BASKERVILLE, STEPHEN W., ADMAN, PETER & BEEDHAM, KATHERINE F. 'Praefering a Whigg to a whimsical: the Cheshire election of 1715 reconsidered', *Bulletin of the John Rylands University Library of Manchester* 74(3), 1992, 139-68. Based on poll books of 1710 and 1715; includes biographical notes on Cheshire politicians.

BASKERVILLE, S.W. 'The political behaviour of the Cheshire clergy, 1705-1752', *Northern history* 23, 1987, 74-97.

DAVIES, C. STELLA. *The agricultural history of Cheshire, 1750-1850.* Cm.S., 3rd series 10. 1960. General study; includes useful bibliography, list of enclosure awards, 1785 land tax returns for Bruern Stapleford, survey of Tiverton 1773, rental of Dorfold and Croxton, 1773, Wilbraham estate correspondence, 1745-8, Macclesfield enclosure award, 1796-1804, *etc.*

WALKER, R.B. 'Religious changes in Cheshire 1750-1850', *Journal of ecclesiastical history* 17, 1966, 77-94.

SCARD, GEOFFREY H. *Squire and tenant: life in rural Cheshire, 1760-1900.* History of Cheshire 10. Chester: Cheshire Community Council, 1981.

HARROP, S.A. 'Literacy and educational attitudes as factors in the industrializing of north-east Cheshire, 1760-1830', in STEPHENS, W.B. ed. *Studies in the history of literacy: England and North America.* Leeds: the University, 1983, 37-53.

ADDY, J. 'Bishop Porteus' visitation of the Diocese of Chester, 1778', *Northern history* 13, 1977, 175-98. Uses the visitation returns to describe the state of the Diocese.

EVANS, ERIC J. 'Landownership and the exercise of power in an industrializing society; Lancashire and Cheshire in the nineteenth century', in GIBSON, RALPH & BLINKHORN, MARTIN, eds. *Landownership and power in modern Europe.* Harper Collins, 1981, 145-63.

LAWTON, R. 'Population trends in Lancashire and Cheshire, from 1801', *H.S.L.C.* 114, 1962, 189-213. Based on the census.

KAIN, R.J.P. 'Farming in Cheshire circa 1840: some evidence from the tithe files', *L.C.A.S.* 82, 1983, 22-57.

LEE, J.M. *Social leaders and public persons: a study of county government in Cheshire since 1888.* Oxford: Clarendon Press, 1963.

11

Local histories, *etc.*

A listing of parochial studies would occupy another volume, and cannot be attempted here. The works that are listed here are either of particular importance to the genealogist, and based on genealogical sources, or are otherwise of general interest. Mention must first be made of:

Township packs. Chester: Cheshire Libraries Arts and Archives, 1990- . This series aims to provide resource materials as a starting point for the history of particular townships, e.g. directory entries, the relevant extract from Ormerod's *History*, maps, illustrations, *etc.* There is one pack for each township.

Extracts from parish records, hearth tax returns, trade directories, *etc.,* are also to be found in a series of local histories by Frank Latham. The earliest of these was:

LATHAM, FRANK A. *Alpraham: the history of a Cheshire village.* [Alpraham]: Local History Group, 1969. Further volumes cover Tilston Fearnall, Tiverton, Tarporley, Cuddington and Sandiway, Tattenhall, Christleton, Farndon, Barrow, Tarvin, Frodsham, Bunbury, Delamere, and Vale Royal.

Appleton
See Aston

Aston
FOSTER, CHARLES F. 'The landowners and residents of four North Cheshire townships in the 1740s', *H.S.L.C.* **141,** 1992, 101-205. Study of the estate records of Aston, Appleton, Great Budworth, and Crowley; includes various lists of landowners and tenants, *etc.*

Bucklow Hundred
KNEEBONE, H.R. *Pre-industrial South Halton, 1700-1850.* Halton historical publications **13.** Halton: Halton Borough Council, 1988. Based on land tax assessments, tithe awards, and census returns of Bucklow and Rocksavage Hundreds.

Castle Northwich
MACGREGOR, A.J. *Old Castle Northwich.* Northwich: Vale Royal Historical Publications, 1992. Includes names of landowners and occupiers, 17-19th c., with full transcript of 1841 census.

Chester
ALLDRIDGE, NICHOLAS. 'The mechanics of Cheshire: irrigation and economy in early modern Chester', in REED, MICHAEL, ed. *English towns in decline 1350-1800.* Working papers 1. Leicester: University of Leicester Centre for Urban History, 1986, unpaginated.

JONES, W.J. 'The Exchequer of Chester in the last years of Elizabeth I', in SLAVIN, A.J., ed. *Tudor men and institutions: studies in English law and government.* Baton Rouge: Louisiana State University, 1972, 123-70.

ALLDRIDGE, NICK. 'Loyalty and identity in Chester parishes, 1540-1640', in WRIGHT, S.J., ed. *Parish, church and people: local studies in lay religion, 1350-1750.* Hutchinson, 1988, 85-124.

WOODWARD, D.M. *The trade of Elizabethan Chester.* Occasional papers in economic and social history **4.** Hull: University of Hull Publications, 1970.

MORRIS, RUPERT H. *The siege of Chester 1643-1646.* ed. P.H. Lawson. Chester: G.R. Griffith, 1923. Issued as *J.C.A.H.S.* N.S., **25.** 1923. Includes extracts from a return of householders with corn supplies, 1645/6, extracts from parish registers, *etc.*

Congleton
STEPHENS, W.B., ed. *History of Congleton.* Manchester: Manchester University Press, 1970.

Crewe
CHALONER, W.H. *The social and economic development of Crewe 1780-1823.* Economic history series **14.** Manchester: Manchester University Press, 1950.

Crowley
See Aston

Etchells
See Northenden

Frodsham
BEAMONT, WILLIAM. *An account of the ancient town of Frodsham in Cheshire.* Warrington: Percival Pearse, 1881. Includes accounts of old Frodsham families, monumental inscriptions, *etc.*

DODD, J. PHILLIP. 'The population of Frodsham manor, 1349-50', *H.S.L.C.* **131**, 1982, 21-33. Based on ministers' accounts.

Great Budworth
See Aston

Hale
DORE, R.N. *A history of Hale, Cheshire: from Domesday to dormitory.* Altrincham: John Sherratt and Son, 1972. Good modern history, with notes on sources, and an abbreviated pedigree showing the descent of the Barons of Dunham.

Hyde
MIDDLETON, THOMAS. *Annals of Hyde and district, containing historical reminiscences of Denton, Haughton, Dukinfield, Mottram, Longdendale, Bredbury, Marple, and the neighbouring townships.* Manchester: Cartwright and Rattray, 1809. Includes six chapters on 'old halls and families', *etc., etc.*

Knutsford
YARWOOD, BOB. 'Knutsford families, 1280-1580', *N.C.F.H.* **2**(2), 1973, 8-10 & 5. Based on the parish register.

Macclesfield
DAVIES, C.STELLA, ed. *A history of Macclesfield.* Manchester: Manchester University Press, 1961.
MALMGREEN, GAIL. *Silk town: industry and culture in Macclesfield, 1750-1835.* Hull: Hull University Press, 1985.

Nantwich
HALL, JAMES. *A history of the town and parish of Nantwich, or WichMalbank, in the County Palatine of Chester.* Nantwich: T.Johnson, 1883. Includes manorial descents, monumental inscriptions, parish register extracts, lists of clergy, family histories and pedigrees, *etc., etc.*
KITCHING, C.J. 'Fire disasters and fire relief in sixteenth-century England: the Nantwich fire of 1583', *Bulletin of the Institute of Historical Research* **54**, 1981, 171-87.
WYATT, GRACE M. 'Nantwich and Wybunbury, 1680-1819: a demographic study of two

Cheshire parishes, *H.S.L.C.* **139**, 1990, 1-30. Based on parish registers.
WYATT, GRACE. 'Population change and stability in a Cheshire parish during the eighteenth century', *Local population studies* **43**, 1989, 47-54. Study of surnames in Nantwich, based on parish registers.

Newbold Astbury
CARTLIDGE, J.E.G. *Newbold Astbury and its history.* Congleton: Thomas Gordon, 1915. Reprinted Congleton: Old Vicarage Publications, 1985.

Northenden
GROVES, JILL. *The impact of Civil War on a community: Northenden and Etchells in Cheshire 1642-1660.* Sale: Northern Writers Advisory Service, 1992. Includes much information on the Tatton family of Wythenshawe Hall (including pedigree, 16-17th c.) and pedigree of Brereton of Ashley, 17th c.

Rocksavage Hundred
See Bucklow Hundred

Sandbach
EARWAKER, J.P. *The history of the ancient parish of Sandbach, Co. Chester, including the two chapelries of Holmes Chapel and Goostrey, from original records.* Hansard Publishing Union, 1890. Reprinted Didsbury: E.J. Morten, 1972. Includes lists of incumbents, extracts from parish registers, pedigrees, monumental inscriptions, *etc.*

Stockport
HEGINBOTHAM, HENRY. *Stockport ancient and modern.* 2 vols. Sampson Low, Marston, Searle & Rivington, 1882-92. Includes much information on local families, biographical notes on rectors, discussion of the parish registers, monumental inscriptions, *etc.*
McKENNA, SHIRLEY & NUNN, CATHY. *Stockport in the mid-17th century (1660-1669).* Stockport: Metropolitan Borough of Stockport for Stockport Historical Society, 1993. Based on probate records, the parish registers, hearth tax returns, etc. Includes a list of probate records.

Wallasey

MULLINEUX, ERNEST E. 'A demographic study of two adjoining Wirral parishes in the eighteenth century,' *Cheshire history* 33, 1994, 13-24. Study based on the parish registers of Wallasey and West Kirby.

West Kirby
See Wallasey

Wybunbury
See Nantwich

Diaries

Diaries are important historical sources, and many are in print. Sometimes they contain many names, and can be of considerable genealogical value. Three are of particular importance for Cheshire:

CRAWFURD, GIBBS PAYNE. 'The diary of George Booth of Chester, and Katherine Howard, his daughter, of Boughton, near Chester, 1707-1764,' *J.C.A.H.S.* 28(1), 1928, 5-96. Includes many notes on deaths, also memorial inscriptions and wills of Booth and Howard, and folded pedigree, 16-19th c., showing relationship of Booth, Howard, Proby and Crawfurd.

MARTINDALE, ADAM. *The life of Adam Martindale, written by himself,* ed. Richard Parkinson. Cm.S., O.S., 4. 1845. 17th c.

ADDY, JOHN, ed. *The diary of Henry Prescott, Ll.B., deputy registrar of Chester Diocese.* L.C.R.S., 127. 1987. v.1. 1704-1711. To be continued. Mentions many names of clergy and laymen.

For the diary of Thomas Cartwright, Bishop of Chester, see section 12A below.

2. BIBLIOGRAPHY AND ARCHIVES

A. General

This bibliography is primarily concerned with genealogical source material, and is not intended as a comprehensive listing of Cheshire historical works. It may be complemented by the selective, but valuable:

WALSH, AUDREY G. & ALLAN, ADRIAN R. *The history of the County Palatine of Chester: a short bibliography and guide to sources,* ed. Brian E. Harris. Chester: Cheshire Community Council Publication Trust, 1983.

A much more extensive, but now very outdated bibliography is:

COOKE, JOHN H. *Bibliotheca Cestriensis, or, a biographical account of books, maps, plates, and other printed matter relating to . . . the County of Chester, also giving in many instances, a short biographical account of the authors, together with a list of the commissions issued and depositions taken by the Court of Exchequer for this ancient county palatine, a list of the inclosure awards filed with the Clerk of the Peace, a list of coins struck at the Chester mint, a list of all newspapers published within the County, an account, written in 1593 of all salt works at the Northwych from the beginning.* Warrington: Mackie & Co., 1804. Includes list of Cheshire tokens.

For a much briefer listing, covering both Cheshire and Lancashire, see:

REID, T.D.W. *North West England.* Readers guide, 41. Library Association Public Libraries Group, 1982.

A useful guide to local studies material in Cheshire libraries and archives is provided by:

Local studies manual. Chester: Cheshire County Council, 1992.

The catalogue of an important local collection is printed in:

FIRBY, N.K., ed. *Author catalogue of the Lancashire and Cheshire Antiquarian Society library in the Manchester Central Library.* Manchester: the Society, 1968.

For current publications, see:

'Review of periodical literature and occasional publications, *Northern history* 5- , 1970- .

Accessions to a number of archive repositories were reported for a few years in:

'Archive accessions,' *Northern history* **5-14,** 1970-78.

There is an extensive network of libraries, museums, record offices, and societies concerned with the history of Cheshire. These are listed in the indispensable:

WYKE, TERRY & RUDYARD, NIGEL. *The directory of local studies in North West England.* Manchester: Bibliography of North West England, 1993. This covers Lancashire, Cumberland and Westmorland as well as Cheshire.

See also:

EDDISON, MICHAEL. 'Local studies in Cheshire', *Manchester region history review* **4**(2), 1990/1, 47-50. General discussion of library services.

STEWART-BROWN, RONALD. 'The genealogist in Cheshire', *Genealogists' magazine* **7**(8), 1936, 393-400. Lecture on resources, both printed and manuscript. Now outdated, but may still be useful.

B. Particular Institutions. General

Cheshire Record Office

Cheshire Record Office houses one of the major collections of Cheshire archives. Its records are listed in:

WILLIAMS, CAROLINE M., ed. *Guide to the Cheshire Record Office (and Cheshire Diocesan Record Office).* [Chester]: Cheshire County Council Libraries, Arts and Archives, 1991.

WILLIAMS, CAROLINE. 'A brief outline of sources available for Cheshire studies at the County Record Office, Chester', *Cheshire history* **34**, 1994, 28-30

BEAZLEY, ELIZABETH E. 'Cheshire history from the County records', *Cheshire historian* **10**, 1960, 25-9.

ROWE, F.G.C. 'Cheshire county records', *Cheshire historian* **3**, 1953, 27-33.

For new accessions, see:

'Cheshire Record Office list of accessions ...', *Cheshire history newsletter* **1-13**, 1971-7, *passim.* Continued in *Cheshire history* **2-11**, 1978-83, *passim.*

Cheshire Record Office holds the archives of the Diocese of Chester, founded in 1561. For a general survey of these records, see:

THACKER, A.T. 'Chester Diocesan records and the local historian', *H.S.L.C.* **130**, 1981, 149-85. Since 1541.

Chester City Record Office

CHESTER CITY RECORD OFFICE. *Archives and records of the city of Chester: a guide to the collections in the Chester City Record Office.* Chester: Council of the City of Chester, 1985.

John Rylands Library

A major collection of Cheshire archives is also held by the John Rylands Library of the University of Manchester. A general survey of its holdings is provided by:

CLAYTON, DOROTHY J. 'Sources for the history of North-West England in the John Rylands University Library of Manchester', *Bulletin of the John Rylands University Library of Manchester* **71**(2), 1989, 181-203.

See also:

LORD, EVELYN. 'A brief outline of sources available for the study of Cheshire history in the John Rylands Library, Manchester', *Cheshire history* **32**, 1993, 20-23. Includes a brief summary of the major collections of family archives.

A number of other works on the John Rylands are listed in the 3rd edition of *English genealogy: an introductory bibliography.*

Public Record Office

Many Cheshire records are held in London at the Public Record Office. For a detailed listing of a very wide range of Cheshire and Lancashire documents, see:

SELBY, WALFORD D. *Lancashire and Cheshire records preserved in the Public Record Office, London.* L.C.R.S. **7-8.** 1882-3.

This is supplemented by:

B[ENNETT], J.H.E. 'Cheshire references in Palmer's index', *C.Sf.* 3rd series **21**, 1926, 3-5.

For records of the Palatinate see section 14 below. Other guides to the Public Record Office are listed in *English genealogy: an introductory bibliography.*

15

C. Particular Institutions. Local

Altrincham

FITZPATRICK, GILLIAN. 'Altrincham Library local history collection', *Manchester region history review* 1(2), 1987, 36-40.

Birkenhead

Family history: a guide to the sources available in the Birkenhead Reference Library. Birkenhead: Metropolitan Borough of Wirral, 1989.

Cheadle

Cheadle and district local history: a brief guide to printed works and other sources. Handlist **8**. Stockport: Metropolitan Borough of Stockport Library of Local Studies, 1976.

Chester

The gentle readers guide to 19th century Chester, 1: general sources. [Chester]: Cheshire Libraries and Museums, 1976. Brief bibliography.

KENNETT, ANNETTE M. *Archives and records of the City of Chester: a guide to the collections in the Chester City Record Office.* Chester: Council of the City of Chester, 1985.

New accessions were briefly reported in:
'Chester City Record Office: list of accessions . . .', *Cheshire history newsletter* **1**, 1971, 20; **2**, 1972, 26; **4**, 1973, 27.

More specifically for the genealogist is:
Family history. Source guides 2. Chester: Chester City Council Record Office, [199-]. Guide to records in Chester City Record Office.

For photographs, see:
FISHER, GRAHAM. 'Thirty years of the Chester photographic survey', *Local studies librarian* 12(1), 1993, 11-13.

Lymm

'Lymm collectanea', *L.C.A.S.* **48**, 1932, 181. Lists materials collected by G.B.Thurstan for a parochial history.

'Lymm and District Local History Society: printed materials, *etc.,* held in Lymm Library', *Q.J.L.D.* 3(4), 1950, 1-16.

Marple

Marple and district local history: a brief guide to printed works and other sources. Handlist 6. Stockport: Library of Local Studies, 1975.

Stockport

Genealogy in Stockport: a guide to sources in the Heritage Library. 5th ed. Handlist 14. Stockport: Stockport Libraries, 1994.

A brief introduction and guide to the Library of Local Studies. Handlist 7. Stockport: Metropolitan Borough of Stockport, 1984. Brief bibliography of Stockport.

HAMILTON, LYNNE & MYERSCOUGH, MARGARET. 'Local studies in Stockport', *Manchester region history review* 3(2), 1989/90, 47-50. Describes the collection of Stockport local studies library.

'How to locate archives mentioned in Stockport Library', *N.C.F.H.* 10(1), 1983, 8-10.

Local history and reference material on microfilm. Handlist 15. Stockport: Metropolitan Borough of Stockport Recreation and Culture Division, 1980. Lists antiquarian collections, archives, genealogical records, (census etc.) newspapers, etc.

'Unpublished work on Stockport and neighbourhood', *Cheshire history newsletter* **8**, 1975, 25-7. Primarily a list of theses.

Tameside

Tameside straddles the old Lancashire/ Cheshire border; it incorporates Dukinfield, Hyde, Longdendale and Stalybridge, formerly in Cheshire.

Tameside bibliography. Rev. ed. Stalybridge: Tameside Leisure Services, Libraries & Heritage Division, 1992.

LOCK, ALICA. 'Tameside Local Studies Library', *Manchester Region history review* 1(1), 1987, 34-8

D. Antiquarian Collections, *etc.*

Broster

'The Broster mss', *C.Sf.* 3rd series **16**, 1921, 67. Brief list of an antiquary's collection.

Earwaker

HALL, JAMES. 'Report on the Earwaker Museum Library, Chester', *J.C.A.H.S.* N.S., **17**, 1910, 97-106.

Hankinson

FRANCIS, JEAN. 'The Hankinson manuscripts', *N.C.F.H.* 1(4), 1972, 9. Description of an antiquarian's collection in the John Rylands Library; includes many monumental inscriptions, and much on the Hankinson family.

Johnston

LINDO, JANE. 'Brief summary of legal documents and correspondence originating mainly from the records of John Walkins Johnston, solicitor of 8, Vernon Street, Stockport (but including several other sources) dated approx. 1860-1890', *F.H.S.C.J.* 16(1), 1986, 19-20; 16(2), 1986, 11-13; 16(3), 1907, 4-5; 16(4), 1987, 14-16; 17(1), 1987, 16-17.

Leycester

HORWOOD, ALFRED J. 'Tabley House, the seat of the Right Honourable the Lord de Tabley', in HISTORICAL MANUSCRIPTS COMMISSION. *First report ...* C55, H.M.S.O., 1974, appendix, 46-50. Describes papers of the Leycester family - primarily antiquarian collections on county history, but also estate papers, *etc.*

D. Family History Societies

Family history societies provide important resources for their members - and, indeed, for all genealogists. The Cheshire societies have published a great deal of information, especially on the census, on monumental inscriptions, and in their journals; this material is listed at appropriate points below. The history of these societies is briefly outlined in.

CHADWICK, PETER. 'Cheshire's three family history societies - and journals', *South Cheshire Family History Society quarterly journal* 11, 1993, 11.

For the activities of particular societies, see:

JOHNSON, PETER T. 'Guest society: South Cheshire Family History Society', *Family tree magazine* 9(12), 1993, 9.

DEWDNEY, PETER. 'The Family History Society of Cheshire', *Family tree magazine* 6(11). 1990, 21.

The compilation of registers of members' interests is an important part of the work of family history societies. These enable you to make contact with others who may be researching the same lines as yourself. See:

MOILLIET, DIANA. *Family History Society of Cheshire register of members interests.* [ ]: F.H.S.C., 1993.

See also:

British Isles genealogical register: Cheshire. Birmingham: Federation of Family History Societies, 1994.

Much older registers are provided by:

BRATT, CLIFFORD. *The Family History Society of Cheshire calendar of members interests.* Upton: F.H.S.C., 1976.

FRANKCOM, DOROTHY & LITTON, PAULINE M. *Combined register of members interests, 1981.* [ ]: Family History Society of Cheshire; North Cheshire Family History Society; Liverpool Family History Society; Rossendale Society for Genealogy and Heraldry, Lancashire, 1981.

3. PERIODICALS AND NEWSPAPERS

There are many periodicals of interest to the Cheshire genealogist. Those published by the local family history societies are of considerable value, especially for current information. However, the history of these journals is fairly complex. The earliest two were:

The Family History Society of Cheshire [journal]. 1969-73.
Family History Society of Cheshire Northern Region news bulletin. 1970-71. 6 issues.
Continued by: *The North Cheshire family historian: the journal of the North Cheshire region of the Family History Society of Cheshire.* 1972-3.
These merged in 1974 to become:
Cheshire family historian. 6 vols. Chester: F.H.S.C., 1974-5.
This was continued by:
The Family History Society of Cheshire [journal]. [ ]: F.H.S.C; 1975- . (Commences with vol.5).
The North Cheshire group of the F.H.S.C. seceded to form a separate society; their journal is:
North Cheshire family historian. North Cheshire Family History Society, 1977- .
Finally a new society was formed in 1990 for South Cheshire; its journal is:
South Cheshire Family History Society quarterly journal. 1990-93. Continued by *Cheshire genealogist: quarterly journal of the South Cheshire Family History Society.* 1993- .
There are three major county-wide historical journals for Cheshire. Two of these cover Lancashire as well, and all include a great deal of information for the genealogist (much of which is listed in this bibliography). These journals, with their indexes, are as follows:
Historic Society of Lancashire and Cheshire proceedings and papers. 1848/9- .
Subsequently (from 1855) *Transactions of the* . . .
This is indexed in:
BEAZLEY, F.C. *Index of volumes I to LI, 1849-1900, of the Transactions of the Historic Society of Lancashire and Cheshire.* Liverpool: Thomas Brakell, 1904. Supplement to *H.S.L.C.* **54;** N.S., **18,** 1904.

'Index to papers and communications, vols LII to end including vol. LXI', *H.S.L.C.* **61;** N.S., **25,** 1909, 229-30.
'Index to volumes LXII (1910) to LXX1 (1919)', *H.S.L.C.* **74;** N.S., **38,** 1922, 198-209.
'Index to volumes 72 (1920) to 85 (1933)', *H.S.L.C.* **86,** 1935, 11936.
DICKINSON, R. 'General index, vols.86-97 (1934-45)', *H.S.L.C.* **99,** 1947, 119-29.
'General index, vols.98-110 (1946-58)' *H.S.L.C.* **110,** 1958, 205-9.
'Ten year index, vols.111-120 (1959-68)', *H.S.L.C.* **120,** 1968, 161-8.
'Decennial index, vols. 121-128 and occasional vols. 1 and 2', *H.S.L.C.* **130,** 1981, 213-21.
'Decennial index, vols. 130-138 (1981-1989)', *H.S.L.C.* **139,** 1990, 219-29.

Transactions of the Lancashire and Cheshire Antiquarian Society. 1883- .
This is indexed in:
GARRATT, MORRIS. 'An index of the principal contents of *Transactions,* vol.1 (1883)-vol. 80 (1979)', *L.C.A.S.* **82,** 1983, 169-282.
GARRATT, MORRIS. 'An index to the supplementary contents of *Transactions.* vol.1 (1883)-vol. 80 (1979)', *L.C.A.S.* **83,** 1985, 199-259.
There are also decennial indexes, which are not superseded by Garratt:
'General index ...', *L.C.A.S.* **10,** 1892, 280-338; **20,** 1903, 302-48; **40,** 1925, 265-327; **41,** 1926, 139-56; **51,** 1937, 227-309; **60,** 1948, 197-287; **70,** 1960, 103-89; **80** 1979, 96-156.

Journal of the Architectural, Archaeological and Historic Society for the county, city and neighbourhood of Chester. Chester: the Society, 1849-85. Continued by: *Journal of the Chester Archaeological and Historic Society.* 1887- . Title varies. This is indexed in:
Subject indexes to the old series (vols 1-3, 1849-1885) and the new series (vols 1-18, 1887-1911) of the Journal of the Chester and North Wales Archaeological and Historic Society. Chester: G.B. Griffith, 1912.
VARLEY, W.J., & VARLEY, JOAN. *Subject-index and index of authors to volumes 18-28 (1911-1929) of the new series of the Journal of the Chester and North Wales Architectual, Archaeological and Historic Society.* Chester: G.R. Griffith, 1929.

18

There are also two major record publishing societies, both of which cover Lancashire as well as Cheshire. Many of their publications are listed in this bibliography. For a full list of the publications of the Chetham Society, see:

CROSBY, ALAN G. *A society with no equal: the Chetham Society, 1843-1993.* Cm.S., 3rd series 37. 1993. Includes old series, new series and third series publications.

See also:

General index to the remains, historical and literary, published by the Chetham Society, vols. I-XXX. [ ]: Chetham Society, 1863. Ditto, covering vols XXXI-CXIV, published 1893.

For Lancashire and Cheshire Record Society publications, see:

HARRIS, BRIAN E. 'History of the Society & guide to publications, volumes I-CXVII, 1878-1977, *L.C.R.S.,* 118, 1978, separately paginated.

There are also a number of other county-wide journals, including several of the 'notes and queries' type, which print numerous extracts from genealogical sources (the *Cheshire sheaf* was particularly prolific in this regard). The range of journals available is as follows:

Advertiser notes and queries. Stockport: Advertiser Office, 1882-5. Continued by *Cheshire notes and queries ...* 1886-1911. The latter is described as 'new series' from 1886; however a 'new' new series commenced with v.1 in 1896 - very confusing!

The Cheshire historian. 10 vols, Chester: Cheshire Community Council, 1951-60. This is indexed in 'The Cheshire historian 1951-1960', *Cheshire historian* 10, 1960, 57-70, and continued by:

Cheshire round. Chester: Cheshire Community Council, 1961-9. Continued by:

Cheshire history newsletter. [Chester]: Cheshire Community Council, County Local History Committee, 1971-7. 13 issues. Title varies; indexed in GARRATT, MORRIS. 'Cheshire history newsletter, no.1, September 1971- no.13, September 1977: a subject index', *Cheshire history* 2, 1978, 59-66, and continued by:

Cheshire history. [Chester]: Cheshire Community Council Lical History Committee, 1978- .

The Cheshire sheaf, being local gleanings, historical & antiquarian, from many scattered fields. 1st series (3 vols.) 1880-86. New series (1 vol.) 1895. 3rd series (60 vols.) 1896-1965. 4th series (6 vols.) 1966-69. 5th series (2 vols.) 1977-8.

Lancashire and Cheshire antiquarian notes. 2 vols. Leigh: Chronicle Office, 1885-6.

The Lancashire and Cheshire historian. 3 issues. Macclesfield: [ ], 1965-7.

Local gleanings: an archaeological & historical magazine chiefly relating to Lancashire & Cheshire. Manchester: E.Cornish, 1879-80. Vol.1 and part of vol.2 only published.

The Palatine note-book, for 18--, for the intercommunication of antiquaries, bibliophiles, and other investigators into the history and literature of the counties of Lancashire, Chester, &c. 5 vols. Manchester: J.E. Cornish, *et al,* 1881-4.

Local history journals

There are a number of historical journals devoted to particular places in Cheshire. The list which follows is selective.

Bowdon

The Bowdon sheaf. [Bowdon]: Bowdon History Society, 1983- .

Burton

The Burton and South Wirral Local History Society Bulletin. 1977- . Originally the Burton and District Local History Society. Includes little of genealogical interest.

Chester

Chester local history news. Chester: Chester City Record Office, 1991- . Brief notes on local historical news, events, new books, *etc.*

Frodsham

Frodsham and District Local History Group journal. 1986- . Indexed in:

'Index of subjects' *Frodsham & District Local History Group journal* 17, 1994, 21-2. Index to vols.1-16.

Knutsford

Journal of the Knutsford Historical and Archaeological Association. Knutsford: the Association, 1972- . Title varies.

Lymm

Quarterly journal of the Lymm and District Local History Society. 1977-84. Continued by *Journal of the Lymm and District Local History Society.* 1985- . Indexed in:

'An index of materials contained in the publications of the Lymm and District Local History Society', *Q.J.L.D.* 4(1), 1980, 1-15.

'Contents list ... vol.4, part 1, November 1980 to vol.7, part II, February 1984', *J.L.D.L.H.S.* 3(2), 1987, 9-10.

Malpas

Malpas history. Malpas: Malpas Field Club History Group, 1983-8. 9 issues.

Poynton

Poynton Local History Society newsletter. 1980- . Indexed in:

'Poynton Local History Society newsletter index to nos. 1-15', *Poynton Local History Society newsletter.* 15, 1989, 15-19.

Stockport

Stockport heritage. Manchester: Stockport Heritage Publications, 1987- . Brief articles, notes and news. Popular.

Wirral

Wirral notes and queries, being local gleanings, historical and antiquarian, relating to the Hundred of Wirral from many sources. Birkenhead: Willmer Bros. and Co., 1892-3. 2 vols.

Newspapers.

Newspapers are valuable sources of genealogical information - especially their births, marriages and deaths columns. A comprehensive listing of Cheshire newspapers is provided in:

COWLEY, RUTH. *Newsplan: report of the Newsplan project in the northwestern region, September 1986-January 1990.* Lancashire bibliography 12. British Library, 1990. This also covers Lancashire and the Isle of Man, and supersedes SMITH, R.E.G., ed. *Newspapers first published before 1900 in Lancashire, Cheshire and the Isle of Man: a union list of holdings in libraries and newspaper offices within that area.* Library Association, Reference Special and Information Section, 1964.

See also:

JACKSON, MICHAEL. 'Cheshire local newspapers', *N.C.F.H.* 11(3), 1984, 91-4; 11(4), 1984, 109-12. Includes a concise list.

For an index to more recent newspapers, see:

Chester newspaper index, 1955-59. Chester Public Library Committee, 1964. A further volume covers 1960-64, published 1970.

4. OCCUPATIONAL INFORMATION

There are many works providing biographical information on persons of particular occupations; these are listed here. For clergymen, see section 12, Members of Parliament, sheriffs, justices of the peace, etc; section 11, teachers and students, section 13. This list complements the list in my *Occupational sources for genealogists*. Historical accounts of particular occupations which do not include genealogical information are, in general, not listed here.

Alehouse Keepers

H., K.D. 'Alesellers recognizances, Hundred of Nantwich', *C.Sf.* 4th series **4**, 1969, 14-16. Lists alesellers.

IRVINE, WM. FERGUSSON. 'The Wirral licencing sessions for 1561', *Wirral notes and queries* 1, 1892, 80-82. Lists alehouse keepers.

MACGREGOR, A.J. *The alehouses and alehouse keepers of Cheshire, 1629-1828.* Caupona publications 4. Northwich: MacGregor, 1992. Comprehensive listings from alehouse recognizances.

MACGREGOR, A.J. *The licensees of the public houses of Vale Royal.* Northwich: Vale Royal Historical Publications, 1990.

MACGREGOR, A.J. *The public houses of Northwich: an historical guide.* 2nd ed. Northwich: Vale Royal Historical Publications, 1992.

See also Innkeepers

Apothecaries

RUTTER, JANET AXWORTHY. 'Lifestyle in the Rows with particular reference to a collection of pottery from 11, Watergate Street, Chester', *J.C.A.H.S.* **67**, 1984, 55-75. Includes appendix listing many seventeenth-century apothecaries.

Apprentices

B[ENNETT], J.H.E. 'Some early Chester apprentice indentures', *C.Sf.* 3rd series **31**, 1937, 49-50. 16th c.

BENNETT, J.H.E. 'Chester apprentices, 1557-1646', *C.Sf.* 3rd series **7-8**, 1910-11, *passim.* Lists indentures.

BENNETT, J.H.E. 'Chester apprentice indentures, 1603-1684', *C.Sf.* 3rd series **8**, 1911-13, *passim.* Full abstracts of 60 indentures.

'Chester apprentice indentures 1690-1794', *C.Sf.* 3rd series **13**, 1918, *passim;* **24**, 1929, *passim.*

B[ENNETT], J.H.E. 'Chester apprentice indentures, 1750-1776', *C.Sf.* 3rd series **30**, 1935, 27-60, *passim*

'Apprentices to the Company of Painters, Glaziers, Embroiderers amd Stationers of Chester', *C.Sf.* 3rd series **26**, 1934, *passim.* List, 1566-1866.

See also Book Trades

Archers

HOLLY. 'Cheshire archers at the Scottish wars in 1400', *C.Sf.* 3rd series **18**, 1823, 33-4. Includes list.

'Cheshire archers in the reign of Henry V', *C.Sf.* 3rd series **6**, 1907', *passim.* Muster roll, 1417.

'The Cheshire archers'. *C.Sf.* 3rd series **5**, 1804, 91-3. List of archers, c.1420.

Architects

ADDLESHAW, G.L.O. 'Architects, sculptors, designers and craftsmen, 1770-1970, whose work is to be seen in Chester Cathedral', *Architectural history* **14**, 1971, 74-109. Lists their names and works, *etc.*

Attorneys

AYLETT, PHILIP. 'Attorneys and clients in eighteenth-century Cheshire: a study in relationships 1760-1785', *Bulletin of the John Rylands Library* **69**, 1987, 326-58. General study.

TAYLOR, HENRY. 'Attorneys of the County Palatine court, 1730', *C.Sf.* 3rd series **12**, 1917, 83. List of attorneys sworn. For 1729, see 87-8.

'Chester attornies in 1730', *C.Sf.* 3rd series **26**, 1934, 72-3 & 76. List.

Authors

HANDLEY-TAYLOR, GEOFFREY. *Cheshire, Derbyshire and Staffordshire authors today, being a checklist of authors born in these counties, together with brief particulars of authors born elsewhere who are currently working or residing in these counties ... an assemblage of more than 460 authors together with their addresses and (where applicable) their pseudonyms.* Eddison Press, 1972.

'Cheshire authors', *A.N.Q.* **5**, 1885, 29-30, 43-6, 51-3. List.

'Cheshire bibliography', *C.N.Q.* **7** 1887; **8**, 1888, *passim*. Biographical dictionary of Cheshire authors.

Bakers

'The bakers of Chester, 1703', *C.Sf.* 3rd series **14**, 1919, 56. List

Barber Surgeons

SIMPSON, FRANK. 'The city guilds or companies of Chester, with special reference to that of the barber-surgeons', *J.C.A.A.S.* N.S., **18**, 1911, 98-203. Notes many names, including a list of addresses and stewards of the company, 1606-1911.

Bellfounders

CROSSLEY, FRED. H. 'The bells of Cheshire, to the commencement of the XVIIIth century, with some account of their founders, from documentary evidence and from actual survey', *L.C.A.S.* **58**, 1945-6, 205-44.

CLARKE, J.W. 'Cheshire bells: a detailed survey and history of the bells of the county', *L.C.A.S.* **60**, 1948, 86-116; **61**, 1949, 62-90; **62**, 1950-51, 29-53; **63**, 1952-3, 27-51; **65**, 1955, 48-69; **68**, 1958, 24-44.

EARWAKER, J.P. 'Bell-founders in Lancashire and Cheshire and the adjacent counties in the seventeenth and eighteenth centuries', *H.S.L.C.* **42**; N.S., **6**, 1890, 161-80.

Book Trades

BOSTOCK, R.C. 'The Stationers' Company, London: local extracts from its early records', *C.Sf.* **3**, 1891, *passim*. Lists Cheshire apprentices.

NUTTALL, D. 'The book trade in Cheshire prior to 1850', *Cheshire history* **29**, 1992 6-9. Brief general article.

NUTTALL, D., ed. *The book trade in Cheshire to 1850: a directory*. Book trade in the North West project occasional publications **3**. Liverpool: Liverpool Bibliographical Society, 1992. Lists printers and booksellers *etc*, by place.

STEWART-BROWN, R. 'Provincial booksellers and printers', *Notes and queries* **153**, 1927, 453-4. See also **154**, 1928, 41 & 106. Of Lancashire and Cheshire, 17-19th c.

STEWART-BROWN, R. 'The stationers, booksellers and printers of Chester to about 1800', *H.S.L.C.* **83**, 1931, 101-52. Biographical dictionary.

'Chester booksellers in 1786 and earlier', *C.Sf.* 3rd series **21**, 1926, 70-71. Includes list 1592-1691, from a legal case.

See also Printers and Publishers

Brassfounders

SHERLOCK, ROBERT. 'Chandeliers by Chester brassfounders', *J.C.A.H.S.* **56**, 1969, 37-48. Includes pedigree of Brock of Chester, 18th c.

Bricklayers

SIMPSON, FRANK. 'The city gilds of Chester: the Bricklayers' Company', *J.C.A.H.S.* N.S., **22**, 1915-16, 55-90. Many names; includes list of the Company's aldermen and stewards, 1738-1916.

Building Tradesmen

LAUGHTON, J.W. 'The house that John built: a study of the building of a 17th-century house in Chester', *J.C.A.H.S.* **70**, 1987-8, 99-132. Includes accounts, giving names of many tradesmen engaged to build Robert Whitby's house.

WRIGHT, JEAN M. 'The account books of George Roylance', *N.C.F.H.* **9**(1), 1982, 30-32. Includes list of building tradesmen employed in Macclesfield, 1887-9.

Canal Boatmen

'Census returns: Newton (near Middlewich) 1871 census RG 10/3700', *F.H.S.C.J.* **5**(3), 1976, 8. Returns of canal boatmen.

'Census returns: 1871 ...', *F.H.S.C.J.* **6**(1), 1976, 5-7; **6**(2), 1877, 13; **6**(3), 1977, 8-9; **6**(4), 1977, 12-13; **7**(1), 1977, 7. Canal boatmen at Runcorn.

NEYT, ERNEST. 'Boat people in Cheshire: the 1871 census', *F.H.S.C.J.* **14**(3), 1985, 9-11. Extracts from the returns for Old Rode and Church Lawton.

Cheese Makers

DRIVER, EDMUND. *Cheshire: its cheesemakers, their homes, landlords and supporters*. Bradford: H. Casaubon Derwent, 1909. Includes various lists of prize-winners.

Clockmakers

MOORE, NICHOLAS. *Chester clocks and clockmakers.* Chester: Grosvenor Museum, [1976]. Includes list.

D., A. F.E. 'Some early Chester clockmakers', *C.Sf.* 3rd series **55**, 1960, 24. See also 33, 35 & 38. Brief note.

P., L. 'Chester clockmakers', *C.Sf.* 3rd series **8**, 1911, 37 & 39. List, 17-18th c.

'Cheshire clockmakers', *C.Sf.* 3rd series **6**, 1907, *passim.*

'Chester clock & watchmakers: an ABC', *C.Sf.* 5th series **1-106**, 1976-7, 8 & 11. List, 17-18th c.

HOOLE, JOHN. 'Chester clockmakers', *C.Sf.* 3rd series **28**, 1935, 16-17. List from the 1781 *Chester directory.*

Customers

WRIGHT, JEAN. 'Victorian shopping from Arighi Bianchi', *N.C.F.H.* **8**(4), 1981, 115-18. Includes list of customers of a Macclesfield furniture store.

Cutlers

See Smiths

Embroiderers

See Apprentices

Estate Workers

LAURIE, KEDRUN, ed. *Cricketer preferred: estate workers at Lyme Park, 1898-1946.* Lyme Park: Lyme Park Joint Committee, 1980.

Freemasons

ARMSTRONG, J. *A history of Freemasonary in Cheshire, being a record of all extinct and existing lodges, craft and mark, and royal arch chapters, provincial grand lodges, craft and mark, and provincial grand chapter.* Bro. George Kenning, 1901. Includes various lists of officers; also pedigrees of Egerton, Cambourne, De Tabley, Holme, Warburton, Smith-Barry, and Lee.

ARMSTRONG, JOHN. *The Time Immemorial Lodge at Chester ...* Chester: J. Thomas, 1900. Includes list of members from 1725-1900, *etc.*

RYLANDS, W.H. 'Freemasonary in Lancashire and Cheshire (XVII century)', *H.S.L.C.* **50**, N.S., **14**, 1898, 131-202; **51**, N.S., **15**, 1899, 85-154.

TAYLOR, HENRY, & LAWSON, P.H. *A short history of Freemasonary in Cheshire.* Birkenhead: Willmer Bros., 1925. Includes list of officers from 1725.

Garthweb Weavers

RICHBELL, D.G. 'The garthweb weavers of Sale and Aston-on-Mersey', *Cheshire history* **1**, 1978, 27-30.

Glaziers

See Apprentices

Gold Beaters

MYATT, MAY. 'Some notes on gold beating in Lymm', *J.L.D.L.H.S.* **1**(1), 1985, 11-12. Lists gold beaters, 1920.

Goldsmiths

BALL, T. STANLEY. 'Ancient Chester goldsmiths and their work', *L.C.A.S.* **32**, 1914, 179-200.

RIDGWAY, MAURICE H. *Chester goldsmiths from early times to 1726.* Altrincham: John Sherratt & Son, 1968. Reprinted from *J.C.A.H.S.* **53**, 1966. Includes 'an alphabetical list of Chester goldsmiths, with biographical details and a record of their work'.

RIDGWAY, MAURICE H. *Some Chester goldsmiths and their marks.* Chester: Lowe & Sons, 1973. Includes brief biographical notes.

TAYLOR, HENRY. 'Notes on some mediaeval gold-smiths in Chester', *J.C.A.H.S.* N.S., **4**, 1892, 178-85. Abstracts of 6 medieval deeds.

Heralds

SQUIBB, G.D. 'The deputy heralds of Chester', *L.C.A.H.S.* **56**, 1969, 23-36.

Huntsmen

FERGUSSON, R.E. EGERTON. *The Green Collars: the Tarporley Hunt Club and Cheshire hunting history.* Quiller Press, 1993. Includes extensive list of members 1762-1993.

Innkeepers

MACGREGOR, A.J. *The inns and innkeepers of West Cheshire.* Caupona publications 1. Northwich: The author, 1992.

SIMPSON, FRANK. 'The Royal Oak Inn, Chester', *J.C.A.H.S.* N.S., **27**(1), 1926, 24-36. Includes list of owners or tenants, 17-20th c.

'Custom House Tavern, Watergate Street, Chester', *C.Sf.* 3rd series **51**, 1956, 47; **52**, 1958, 1-4, *passim*. Lists licencees, 17-20th c.

Ironmasters

AWTY, B.G. 'Charcoal ironmasters of Cheshire and Lancashire, 1600-1785', *H.S.L.C.* **109**, 1957, 71-124. Includes pedigree of Hall, Kent and Bridge, 17th c., also Fownes, Cotton, Booth and Bache, 16-18th c., Vernon and Kendall, 18-19th c., with list of customers, 1673 and 1710/11.

Locomotive Engineers

REED, BRIAN. *Crewe locomotive works and its men*. Newton Abbot: David & Charles, 1982. Includes biographical notes on leading engineers *etc.*

Manufacturers

See Merchants

Merchants

WILSON, K. P., ed. *Chester customs accounts 1301-1566*. L.C.R.S. **111**. 1969. Gives names of many merchants and ships' masters paying customs.

BURTON, ALFRED. 'Stockport merchants and manufacturers in 1787', *A.N.Q.* **1**, 1882, 87. List from Tunnicliffe's *Topographical survey of the counties of Stafford, Chester and Lancashire*.

'Stockport merchants and manufacturers in 1787', *C.N.Q.* N.S., **4**, 1899, 177-8. List.

Millers

CALLADINE, ANTHONY, & FRICKER, JEAN. *East Cheshire textile mills*. Royal Commission on the Historical Monuments of England, 1993. General study; names some millers.

Mill Workers

BROOKS, LILIAN. 'Memorial plate, Robert Hall & Son, Kingston Mill, Hyde', *Manchester genealogist*, **18**(1), 1982, 12. Lists those with 25 years service at the mill, 1887.

Mine Owners and Workers, etc.

BURT, ROGER, WAITE, PETER, & BURNLEY, RAY. *The mines of Shropshire and Montgomeryshire, with Cheshire & Staffordshire: metalliferous and associated minerals, 1845-1913*. Exeter: University of Exeter Press, 1990. Includes list of mines, with names of owners and managers.

CHALLINOR, RAYMOND. *The Lancashire and Cheshire mines*. Newcastle-upon-Tyne: Frank Graham, 1972. Extensive general study with good bibliography.

CROFTON, HENRY THOMAS. 'Lancashire and Cheshire coal-mining records', *L.C.A.S.* **7**, 1889, 26-73.

Organists

BRIDGE, JOSEPH C. 'The organists of Chester Cathedral', *J.C.A.H.S.* N.S., **19**, 1912, 63-124. 1541-1877. Brief biographies. Includes folded pedigree of Jewett of Chester, 16-17th c.

HUGHES, T. 'Thomas Bateson, organist of Chester Cathedral', *C.Sf.* **2**, 1883, 133. Lists organists, 1541-1877.

Painters

See Apprentices

Pewterers

'Freeman lists of Chester pewterers, 1476 to 1805', *C.Sf.* 5th series **107-91**, 1977.

Pipemakers

RUTTER, JANET & DAVEY, PETER. 'Clay pipes from Chester', in DAVEY, PETER, ed. *The archaeology of the clay tobacco pipe, III: Britain: the North and West*. British archaeological reports, British series **78**. 1980, 41-272. Includes extensive list of pipemakers, with brief biographical notes.

K., M. 'Chester based pipe makers', *C.Sf.* 5th series **1-106**, 1976-7, 19 & 21-2, 24, 27, 29 & 37. List, 17-18th c.

SPENCE, GEORGE COOPER. 'Notes on clay tobacco pipes and clay pipe makers in Cheshire', *L.C.A.S.* **56**, 1941-2, 45-66.

Plumbers

See Smiths

Police

JAMES, R. W. *To the best of our skill and knowledge: a short history of the Cheshire Constabulary 1857-1957*. Chester: Chief Constable of Cheshire, 1957. Includes list of honours awarded.

Politicians

'Cheshire candidates at the general election, 1885', *C.N.Q.* **6**, 1886, 70-73. Brief biographies.

Printers

NUTTALL, DEREK. *A history of printing in Chester from 1688 to 1865.* Chester: the author, 1969. Includes brief pedigrees of early printers: Broster, Adams, Monk, *etc.*

NUTTALL, D. 'A history of printing in Chester', *J.C.A.H.S.* **54**, 1967, 35-95. Includes pedigree of Broster, 18th c.

See also Book trades

Publishers

HUGHES, THOMAS. 'On Chester literature, its authors and publishers', *Journal of the Architectural, Archaeological and Historic Society for ... Chester* 1(5) 1858, 21-30.

Race Subscribers

'Stockport races', *C.N.Q.* **8**, 1888, 24-5. See also 40-41. List of subscribers to Stockport races, 1783-6.

Rowers

GLASS, J.V.S., & PATRICK, J. MAX. *The Royal Chester Rowing Club: centenary history, 1838-1938.* Liverpool: James Laver, 1939. Includes list of officers 1838-1938, list of winners of the Frost Sculls, 1882-1938, and many other names.

Sailors

WOODWARD, DONALD. 'Ships, masters and shipowners of the Wirral, 1550-1650', *Maritime history* 5(1), 1977, 1-25. Includes various lists of ships, masters and crew, 16-17th c.

Salters

CALVERT, ALBERT, F. *Salt in Cheshire.* E. & F.N. Spon, 1915. Includes many extracts from Northwich documents, giving the names of salters and others connected with the industry.

DIDSBURY, BRIAN. 'Cheshire saltworkers', in SAMUEL, RAPHAEL, ed. *Miners, quarrymen and saltworkers.* Routledge, 1977, 137-204.

Shareholders

CLAYE, WILLIAM. 'Stockport Gas Works: list of original shareholders', *C.N.Q.* **7**, 1887, 287-8.

Shipowners

CRAIG, ROBERT. 'Shipping and shipbuilding in the Port of Chester in the eighteenth and early nineteenth centuries', *H.S.L.C.* **116**, 1964, 39-68. Includes a section on shipowners.

See also Sailors

Ships' Masters

See Merchants and Sailors

Silversmiths

RIDGWAY, MAURICE H. *Chester silver, 1727-1837.* Chichester: Phillimore & Co., 1985. Includes extensive biographical dictionary of silversmiths.

Skinners

SIMPSON, FRANK. 'The city guilds of Chester: the Skinners' and Feltmakers' Company', *J.C.A.H.S.* N.S., **21**, 1914, 77-149. Many names, including list of the Company's aldermen and stewards, 17-20th c.

Smiths

SIMPSON, FRANK. 'The city guilds of Chester: the Smiths', Cutlers' and Plumbers' Company', *J.C.A.H.S.* N.S., **20**, 1913, 5-121. Many names, including a list of the company's aldermen and stewards, 1497-1914.

Soldiers, Militiamen *etc.*

There are many works dealing with military life in Cheshire. The essential and extensive guide to them is:

WYKE, TERRY, and RUDYARD, NIGEL. *Military history in the North West.* Manchester: Bibliography of North West England, 1994.

The listing which follows is not comprehensive; rather, it includes only those works which include lists of names, such as rolls of honour, or other information of direct interest to the genealogist. It is arranged in rough chronological order.

BOSTOCK, A.J. *The chivalry of Cheshire.* Didsbury: Morten, 1980. Includes list of Cheshire men who fought in various late 14th c. campaigns.

R., J. 'Cheshire and Lancashire men in service in France in 1380-1 ', *C.Sf.* 3rd series **33**, 1939, 69-82, *passim.*

DUNS SCOTUS. 'Cheshire and Lancashire men at the Battle of Agincourt, 1415', *C.Sf.* 3rd series **6**, 1907, 12-13. List.

GAMON, G.P. 'The siege of Chester', *C.Sf.* 3rd series **5**, 1904, *passim.* Lists officers of the garrison, and householders, 1645.

'The Royalist rendezvous at Knutsford', *C.Sf.* **3** 1883, 257-8. Lists those absent from the December 1660 muster.

FARRINGTON, A.J. 'Maimed royalist soldiers', *Cheshire round* 1(5), 1966, 138-40. Brief note on petitions to Quarter Sessions for pensions, at the Restoration, 1660.

'Pension petitions from royalist soldiers', *F.H.S.C.J.* **6**(2), 1977, 10-11. Includes list.

'Some Cheshire-born soldiers/militiamen discharged to pension between 1760 and 1854', *Cheshire genealogist* **14**, 1993, 27-8.

GLENDINNING, ALEXANDER MURRAY. 'A deadly disease: the decimation of the Loyal Cheshire Fencibles in Jersey', *Cheshire genealogist* **13**, 1993, 14-16. Lists deaths from disease - probably bubonic plague - in 1795-7.

LEARY, FREDERICK. *The Earl of Chester's Regiment of Yeomanry Cavalry: its formation and service, 1797 to 1897.* Edinburgh: Ballantyne Press, 1898. Includes roll of officers, 1796-1896, and various other lists of officers and men.

PHILPOTT, B. 'The officers of the Chester Volunteer Corps', *N.C.F.H.* **4**(2), 1977, 44. List, 1803.

WILKINSON, MARGARET. 'Dad's army, 1803-1808', *N.C.F.H.* 1(2), 1972, 7 & 9. Muster roll of Sale and Ashton on Mersey Volunteers, 1803.

WILLIAMS, J.R. 'Cheshire veterans of the 31st Foot', *F.H.S.C.J.* **12**(3), 1983, 2-4; **12**(4), 1983, 4-6. Lists recruits, 1808-28.

TAYLOR, BETTY. 'Macclesfield's local militia of 1811', *N.C.F.H.* 18(4), 1991, 121-2. Paylist.

VERDIN, SIR RICHARD. *The Cheshire (Earl of Chester's) Yeomanry, 1898-1967.* Chester: [Cheshire Yeomanry Association], 1971. Includes nominal rolls for 1900/1, 1916, and 1933; also rolls of honour, and lists of officers, 1898-1967.

COOKE, JOHN H. *5,000 miles with the Cheshire Yeomanry in South Africa.* Warrington: Mackie & Co., 1913-14. Includes 'Roll of the 21st Company Imperial Yeomanry', 1899-1902.

CROOKENDEN, ARTHUR. *The history of the Cheshire Regiment in the Great War.* Chester: W.H.Evans, [c.1926]. Includes roll of honour, and list of individuals' honours, *etc.*

DISBROW, E.J.W. *History of the Volunteer Movement in Cheshire, 1914-1920.* Stockport: [ ], 1920. Includes rolls of officers 1916 and 1918, with many other names.

CHURTON, W.A.V. *The war record of the 1/5th (Earl of Chester's) Battalion, the Cheshire Regiment, August 1914-June 1919.* Chester: Phillipson and Golder, 1920. Includes various lists of officers and men.

DORNING, H. *The history of no.3 (Hale) Platoon, 'A' Company 1st Volunteer Battalion, the Cheshire Regiment: a humble record of war service, 1914-1919.* Manchester: George Faulkner & Sons, 1920. Includes list of members.

SIMPSON, FRANK. *The Chester Volunteers, with special reference to 'A' Company, 3rd Volunteer Battalion the Cheshire Regiment (1914-1920)* Chester: Courant Press, n.d. Includes list of officers commissioned, 1916, and roll of N.C.O.'s and other ranks 1914-20.

Soldiers died in the Great War, part 27: The Cheshire Regiment. HMSO, 1921. Reprinted Chippenham: Picton, 1988.

SMITH, CHARLES. *War history of the 6th Battalion the Cheshire Regiment.* [ ]: 6th Cheshire Old Comrades Association, 1932. Includes roll of honour, 1914-18.

COMMONWEALTH WAR GRAVES COMMISSION. *The War dead of the Commonwealth: the register of the names of those who fell in the 1939-1945 war and are buried in cemeteries and churchyards in the county of Cheshire.* Commonwealth War Grave Commission, 1961. Reprinted with amendments 1986.

SPENCE, J.C. *They also serve: the 39th Cheshire Battalion, Home Guard.* Manchester: C. Nicholls & Co., 1945. Includes various lists of men.

CROOKENDEN, ARTHUR. *The history of the Cheshire Regiment in the Second World War.* Chester: W.H.Evans Sons, 1949. Includes roll of honour with biographical notes on officers killed, list of decorations and awards, *etc.*

*History of the Cheshire Home Guard, from
L.D.V. formation to stand-down, 1940-1944.*
Aldershot: Gale & Polden, 1950. Gives history
of each unit, with many names - but
unfortunately no index.
*A short history of the units administered by
the Cheshire Territorial and Auxiliary
Forces Association.* Reid-Hamilton, 1951.
Includes brief notices of many units, with
some names, 1939-45.

Stationers
See Apprentices and Book Trades

Tobacconists
G., G.P. 'Early Chester tobacconists', *C.Sf.* 3rd
series **6**, 1907, 49. Lists persons licenced to
sell tobacco in 1633.

Tradesmen
'The register of the Coventry guilds', *C.Sf.* 3rd
series **31**, 1937, 14-20, *passim.* Extracts
relating to Cheshire men, 14-15th c.

Tradesmen's tokens
In an age when currency was in short supply,
many tradesmen issued their own tokens.
Studies of these frequently provide useful
genealogical information. For Cheshire, see:
HEYWOOD, NATHAN. 'Tradesmens' tokens of
Lancashire and Cheshire issued during the
seventeenth century', *L.G.* **1**, 1879-80, 16-18,
201-8 & 281-8. See also 436-8 & 480.
HEYWOOD, NATHAN. Lancashire and Cheshire
tokens of the seventeenth century', *L.C.A.S.*
5, 1887, 64-105. Includes list of issuers.
HEYWOOD, NATHAN. 'Further notes on
Lancashire and Cheshire tokens', *L.C.A.S.*
30, 1912, 65.

5. PARISH REGISTERS AND
OTHER RECORDS OF BIRTHS,
MARRIAGES AND DEATHS.

A. *General*

Registers of births, marriages and deaths are
normally one of the first sources to be
consulted by genealogists. A wide variety of
general works on them are available, and are
listed in my *English genealogy; an
introductory bibliography.* For Cheshire,
original parish registers are listed in:
LANGSTON, B. *Cheshire parish registers: a
summary guide.* 2nd ed. Northwich: F.H.S.C.,
1994. Includes list of monumental inscription
transcripts, and a list of Cheshire townships.
This supersedes N.Lambert's *Index to
Cheshire parish registers, transcripts and
graveyard inscriptions,* published in 1982.
Numerous transcripts of parish registers, both
printed, manuscript, and microfiche, are held
by Manchester Local History Library. These
are listed in:
MANCHESTER & LANCASHIRE FAMILY HISTORY
SOCIETY. *Parish & nonconformist registers
in Manchester Local History Library.*
[Amended ed.] Manchester: Manchester &
Lancashire Family History Society, 1989.
All Cheshire genealogists should be aware of
the Cheshire parish register transcription
project. This is discussed in:
HAIR, P.E.H., & PHILLIPS, C.B. 'The Cheshire
parish register transcription project, 1978-
1989', *Local population studies* **43**, 1989, 55-
61.
For descriptions *etc.,* of an important index
(which is about to be published on microfiche)
to marriage entries in parish registers, see:
MERRELL, B. *Marriage index of Cheshire, 1580-
1837: guide to the index.* Chester: [F.H.S.C.
Northern Region], 1970.
MERRELL, BERTRAM. 'Merrell's marriage index
of Cheshire', *C.F.H.* **4**, 1974, 13-14. See also
6(3), 1977, 18-22 for list of parishes covered.
MERRELL, BERTRAM. 'Bertram Merrell's
marriage index of Cheshire (1580-1837)',
F.H.S.C.J. **19**(4), 1990, 13-16. Lists registers
included.
'Marriage index of Cheshire', *F.H.S.C.J.* **3**(1),
1972, 13. Entries for non-residents of
Cheshire in Merrell's marriage index, 1746-
1829.

'Did they come to Cheshire to be married?',
F.H.S.C.J. 27(3), 1971, 5. Out of county
entries, 1801-36, in Merrell's *Marriage index
of Cheshire.*
For other marriage indexes, see:
LITTON, PAULINE. 'North and East Cheshire
marriage index', *F.H.S.C.J.* 19(4), 1990, 10-12.
Lists parishes covered.
'Mid-Cheshire marriage index', *F.H.S.C.J.*
25(2), 1994, 6.
For 'stray' entries from Cheshire parish
registers, see:
PLANT, W. KEITH. 'List of local strays',
F.H.S.C.J. 13(3), 1984, 12-14, 18-20th c.
There are many other lists of 'strays' in the
various family history society journals *etc.,*
listed in section 3. See, for example:

Adderley, Shropshire
LEA, G. 'Marriages of Cheshire people at
Adderley (Salop), 1756-1810', *F.H.S.C.J.* 4(1),
1973, 7-8.

Ardwick, Lancashire
'St. Thomas, Ardwick marriages, 1742-53',
N.C.F.H. 13(4), 1986, 123. Lists marriages of
Cheshire persons.

Gresford, Denbighshire
'Cheshire strays in North Wales from B.T's in
the National Library of Wales: Gresford',
F.H.S.C.J. 11(1), 1981, 6-8. Marriages, 1801-36;
burials, 1799-1807.

Peak Forest, Derbyshire
'Foreign marriages at Peak Forest Chapel:
extracts', *N.C.F.H.* 4(1), 1977, 7-9. Cheshire
marriages at Peak Forest, Derbyshire,
1747-54.

Stoke on Trent, Staffordshire
CURTIS, A. 'Cheshire folk married at St.Peter's
parish, Stoke on Trent, Staffs.', *F.H.S.C.J.*
3(2), 1972, 7-8. 1813-37.

Warrington, Lancashire
'Cheshire marriages at Warrington', *F.H.S.C.J.*
9(1), 1979, 9. 1760-80.

Whitchurch, Shropshire
CRAIG, J.B. 'Cheshire strays: marriages in
Whitchurch, Shropshire', *F.H.S.C.J.* 9(4),
1980, 18-19. Early 19th c.

Winchester, Hampshire
B[EAZLEY], F.C. 'Lancashire and Cheshire
names in Hampshire', *C.Sf.* 3rd series 6,
1907, 63. Strays from Winchester Cathedral
registers, 17-19th c.

Winwick, Lancashire
BULMER, J. 'Marriages of Cheshire folk at
Winwick parish church (Lancs), 1661-1754',
F.H.S.C.J. 5(2), 1976, 14-15; 5(3), 1976, 14-15.

Wrexham, Denbighshire
BLACKWELL, STEWART. 'Cheshire entries in
Wrexham non-conformist registers',
F.H.S.C.J. 14(3), 1985, 3-5.

Marriage licences and bonds provide a useful
complement to the evidence of parish registers.
Those from the Archdeaconry of Chester
(which covered the whole county) have been
comprehensively listed in:
IRVINE, WM. FERGUSSON, ed. *Marriage licences
granted within the Archdeaconry of Chester,
in the Diocese of Chester.* L.C.R.S. 53, 56,
57, 61, 65, 69, 73 & 77. 1907-24. v.1. 1606-16;
v.2. 1616-24; v.3. 1624-32; v.4. 1639-44; v.5.
1661-7; v.6. 1667-80; v.7. 1680-91; v.8. 1691-
1700.
*Marriage bonds of the ancient Archdeaconry
of Chester now preserved at Chester* L.C.R.S.
82, 85, 97 & 101. 1933-49. Pt.1. 1700-1706/7,
ed. Wm. Assheton Tonge. Pt.2. 1707-11, ed.
Wm Fergusson Irvine. Pt.3. 1711-1715, ed. P.H.
Lawson. Pt.4. 1715-1719, ed. P.H. Lawson.
See also:
R[YLANDS,] J.P. 'Extracts from the marriage
licence books at Chester, 1606 to 1700',
Lancashire and Cheshire antiquarian notes
2, 1886, 15-17. For Lancashire and Cheshire.
L., P.H. 'Chester marriage licences', *C.Sf.* 3rd
series 9, 1913, 79. Brief list, 17-18th c.
For 16th c. marriages, see:
FURNIVALL, FREDERICK J., ed. *Child-marriages,
divorces, and ratifications, &c., in the
Diocese of Chester, A.D. 1561-6: depositions
in trials in the Bishops' Court, Chester,
concerning 1. Child-marriages, divorces and
ratifications. 2. Trothplights. 3. Adulteries. 4.
Affiliations. 5. Libels. 6. Wills. 7.
Miscellaneous matters. Also, entries from the mayors
books, Chester, A.D. 1558-1600.* Early English
Text Society, original series, 108. 1897.

See also:
PRICE, W.H., & MORRIS, CANON. 'Early marriages in the Diocese of Chester', *J.C.A.H.S.* N.S., 6(2), 1899, 217-44.
Nonconformist registers from particular places are listed in the next sub-section. However, events from throughout Yorkshire, Lancashire and Cheshire are recorded in:
HEYWOOD, OLIVER, & DICKENSON, T. *The nonconformist register of baptisms, marriages and deaths ... 1644-1702, 1702-1752, generally known as the Northowram, or Coley register, but comprehending numerous notices of puritans and anti-puritans in Yorkshire, Lancashire, Cheshire, London, &c., with lists of popish recusants, quakers, &c.,* ed. J. Horsfall Turner. Brighouse: J.S. Jowett, 1881.
For vital events of the 19th and 20th c., general background to the system of civil registration is provided by:
DUNN, F.I. *Registration in Cheshire 1538-1987: a brief history to mark 150 years of civil registration, 1837-1987.* Chester: Cheshire County Council, 1987.
See also:
'Civil registration in Cheshire, 1837-1929', *F.H.S.C.J.* 19(2), 1989, 5-13; 19(3), 1990, 5-15. Lists Cheshire Registration Districts.
'The Registrars', *N.C.F.H.* 18(2), 1991, 59-62. Includes list of registration records and their locations in North Cheshire.
For a listing of registration certificates held by the Family History Society of Cheshire, see:
'A collection of birth, marriage and death certificates held by Nantwich group', *F.H.S.C.J.* 19(1), 1989, 20-26.
The births, marriages and deaths columns in newspapers provide much useful information. Some extracts from these have been published in more accessible format:
LAWSON, P.H. 'Births, marriages and deaths [from *Courant* files] *C.Sf.* 3rd series 11-12, 1915-17, *passim*; 26, 1934, 27-33, *passim*
'Local notes from the Liverpool Mercury', *C.Sf.* 3rd series 2, 1934. 83-8, *passim*.
Marriage notices relating to Cheshire folk, 1811.
'Birth, marriages and deaths', *C.Sf.* 3rd series 30, 1935, 63-81, *passim*. For 1815, from Gore's *General advertiser* (Liverpool).

S[TEWART]-B[ROWN], R. 'Marriage and obituary notices for 1817-1819', *C.Sf.* 3rd series 10, 1916, 88-120, *passim.* For Cheshire, from the *Liverpool Courant*.
'Extracts from *Cheshire Courant,* 1820: marriages', *F.H.S.C.J.* 7(4), 1978, 22-3; 8(1), 1978, 13; 8(2), 1979, 13; 8(3), 1979, 17.
Death cards are another potentially useful, but comparatively rare, source. See;
SPEED, ELINOR N.P. 'Some Cheshire death cards', *N.C.F.H.* Nov. 1975, 11-13. List, late 19th-early 20th c., giving addresses, date of death, age and place of burial.

B. *By Locality*

Alderley
CHOICE, LEOPOLD, ed. 'Marriages at Alderley 1629 to 1837', in his *C.P.R.M.* 5. P.P.R.S. 216. Phillimore, 1914, 1-65.

Appleton. Hill Cliff
Burials at the Baptist Chapel at Hill Cliffe in Appleton between 1802 and 1839. Warrington: Liverpool and South-West Lancashire Family History Society, Warrington Group, [1990?]
Children dedicated to God at the Baptist Chapel at Hill Cliffe in Appleton, 1783-1837. Warrington: Liverpool and South West Lancashire Family History Society, Warrington Group, [1990?]

Bebington
SANDERS, FRANCIS & IRVINE, WM. FERGUSSON., eds. *The parish registers of Bebington, Co. Chester, from A.D. 1558 to 1701.* Liverpool: Henry Young and Sons, 1897.
SAMPLES, BARBARA. 'List of local strays taken from Bebington register of marriages', *F.H.S.C.J.* 14(1), 1984, 5. 1816-55.

Bidston
IRVINE, WILLIAM FERGUSSON. *The baptismal, marriage, and burial registers of the parish of Bidston, in the County of Chester, 1581 to 1700.* Birkenhead: Willmer Bros., 1893. Also published in *Wirral notes and queries* 1, 1892, *passim.*

Birkenhead

BEAZLEY, F.C., ed. *The registers of births, deaths and marriages for the chapel of St. Mary's, Birkenhead, 1719-1812.* [ ], 1906. Reprinted from *H.S.L.C.* 58; N.S., 22, 1906, 163-235.

CARR, PHILIP H. 'Seafarers at Birkenhead', *F.H.S.C.J.* 8(4), 1979, 18-19; 9(1), 1979, 17-18. Extracts from parish registers, 1721-1812.

Bosley

CHOICE, LEOPOLD. 'Marriages at Bosley 1729 to 1750', in his *C.P.R.M.* 5. *P.P.R.S.* 216. Phillimore, 1914, 67-8.

Bowdon

ROGERS, COLIN D. 'The Bowdon marriage licences, 1606-1700', *Lancashire and Cheshire historian* 2, 1966, 533-6 & 603-66. General discussion, with some names.

CARR, PHILIP H. 'Strays buried at Bowdon, 100 years ago', *N.C.F.H.* 4(2), 1977, 57-8. Burials for 1876.

'Strays and cuckoos buried at Bowdon, 1877', *N.C.F.H.* 4(4), 1977, 117-9. List.

Bramhall

BAYLISS, ANNE. 'Births, marriages and deaths from a late c18 Bramhall diary', *N.C.F.H.* 7(3), 1980, 85-6. From the diary of Peter Pownall, 1782-88.

Bromborough

ANDERSON, ANNE. *The registers of baptisms, marriages, and burials in the parish of Bromborough in the county of Chester, 1600-1726.* Bromborough: Privately printed, [1962.] Includes biographical notes on clergy, and list of documents in the parish chest, *etc.*

Bruera

IRVINE, WM. FERGUSSON, ed. *The register of Bruera church, formerly in the parish of St. Oswald, Co. Chester 1662-1812.* Parish Register Society 67. 1910. Includes biographical notes on curates.

Burton

BEAZLEY, F.C. 'Notes on the parish of Burton in Wirral', *H.S.L.C.* 59; N.S., 23, 1907, 3-92.

Includes transcript of the parish register, 1538-1725; also monumental inscriptions, lists of clergy, *etc.*

MORRELL, P.F.A. 'The parish registers of the parish of Burton', *J.C.A.H.S.* N.S., 15, 1908, 89-118. General discussion, with some extracts.

MORRELL, P.F.A. *Notes on Burton parish registers.* Chester: G.R. Griffith, 1908. General discussion with list of incumbents and a few extracts.

Capesthorne

CHOICE, LEOPOLD, ed. 'Marriages at Capesthorne, 1722 to 1747', in his *C.P.R.M.* 5. *P.P.R.S.* 216. Phillimore, 1914, 69-70.

Chelford

CHOICE, LEOPOLD, ed. 'Marriages at Chelford 1674 to 1752', in his *C.P.R.M.* 5. *P.P.R.S.* 216. Phillimore, 1914, 71-80.

Chester

BARBER, E. 'The trade and customs of Chester in the 17th and 18th centuries, as shown in some old parish registers', *J.C.A.H.S.* N.S., 17, 1910, 5-18. Includes general discussion of the registers.

Holy Trinity

FARRALL, L.M., ed. *Parish register of the Holy & Undivided Trinity in the City of Chester, 1532-1837.* Chester: G.R.Griffith, 1814. Includes brief biographical notes on prominent parishioners.

'Extracts from Holy Trinity parish registers, Chester', *C.Sf.* 3rd series 53, 1958, *passim.* Brief extracts.

See also Chester. St. Bridget

St. Bridget

B[ENNETT], J.H.E. 'The registers of St. Bridgets, Chester', *C.Sf.* 3rd series 15-18, 1920-23, *passim.* 1560-1642.

'St. Bridget', Cheshire, register of baptisms, 1818-1832', *F.H.S.C.J.* 3(1), 1972, 16-18. Index.

CRUMP, J. HAMERTON, [ed.] 'Randle Holmes's transcripts of Chester parish registers, *C.N.Q.* 7, 1887, 62-5. Extracts, 15-16th c., from St. Bridgets, Holy Trinity, St. Mary on the Hill, and St. Olave.

St. Mary on the Hill

EARWAKER, J.P., & MORRIS, R.H. *The history of the church and parish of St. Mary-on-the-Hill, Chester ...* Love & Wyman: 1898. Includes transcript of the parish register to 1812, also of churchwardens accounts, 16th c., list of churchwardens, many pedigrees, monumental inscription, biographical notes on clergy *etc.*

F., A.J. 'The parish register of St. Mary-on-the-Hill, Chester, 1547-1628', *C.Sf.* 4th series **2**, 1967, *passim.* Transcript.

POLLARD, B. 'St. Mary's-within-the-Walls. Chester, baptism registers, 1600-1700', *F.H.S.C.J.* **7**(1) 1977, 8-9; **7**(2), 1978, 9-10; **7**(3), 1978, 10-11; **7**(4), 1978, 8-9; **8**(1), 1978, 8-10; **8**(2), 1979, 15-16; **8**(3), 1979, 23-4; **8**(4), 1979, 234; **9**(1), 1979, 23-4; **9**(1), 1979, 23-4; **9**(3), 1980, 13-16.

'Index to the register of burials: St. Mary's within the Walls, Chester, 1837-1842', *F.H.S.C.J.* **2**(4), 1971, 9-10; **3**(1), 1972, 10; **3**(2), 1972, 10; **4**(1), 1973, 13-14; **4**(3), 1972, 10-11.

'St. Mary's within the Walls, Chester, baptism registers, 18201824', *F.H.S.C.J.* **2**(1), 1971, 7-9; **2**(2) 1971, 6-9; **2**(3) 1971, 4. Index.

See also Chester, St. Bridget

St. Oswald

'Marriage registers of St. Oswald, Chester', *C.Sf.* 3rd Series **2-3**, 1898-1901, *passim.* Transcript, 1581-1700.

See also Chester, St. Bridget

St. Werburgh

HUGHES, THOMAS, & HUGHES, J.CANN, eds. *The registers of Chester Cathedral, 1687-1812.* Parish Register Society **54**. 1904.

Christleton

G-W., A.A. The registers of Christleton', *C.Sf.* 3rd series **34**, 1941, 67-112, *passim;* **35**, 1948, *passim.* Bishops' transcripts, 1600-1700.

CHOICE, L.E., & CHOICE, J.M., eds. 'Marriages at Christleton, 1697 to 1812', in PHILLIMORE, W.P.W., & CHOICE, LEOPOLD, eds. *C.P.R.M.* **1**. *P.P.R.S.* 111. Phillimore & Co., 1909, 99-118.

Dane Bridge

The burial registers of St.Paul's Church, Dane Bridge, 1849-1956. Northwich: F.H.S.C., Northwich Group, 1994. This (defunct) parish covered part of Northwich town centre.

Disley

CHOICE, LEOPOLD, ed. 'Marriages at Disley, 1591 to 1738', in PHILLIMORE, W.P.W., & CHOICE, LEOPOLD eds. *C.P.R.M.* **1**. *P.P.R.S.* 111. Phillimore & Co., 1909, 1-10.

Dukinfield

FOSTER, IRENE. 'Early marriages recorded at Dukinfield', *N.C.F.H.* **9**(1), 1982, 22-6. List, 1677-1713, from a nonconformist register.

EARWAKER, J.P. 'Extracts from the register of the nonconformist chapel, Dukinfield, kept by the Rev. Samuel Angier, 1677 to 1713', *H.S.L.C.* **33**, 1881, 169-94.

Eastham

SANDERS, FRANCIS, ed. *The parish register of Eastham, Cheshire, from A.D. 1598 to 1700.* Mitchell and Hughes, 1891. Includes list of churchwardens, and transcript of late 17th c. churchwardens' accounts.

Farndon

'Index to the register of baptisms, Farndon parish, 1785-1812', *F.H.S.C.J.* **3**(1), 1972, 12; **3**(4), 1972, 10; **4**(3), 1973, 12-14; *C.F.H.* **6**(3), 1977, 25-6.

'Index: names appearing in Farndon parish registers. Baptism 1813-1838', *F.H.S.C.J.* **1**(2), 1970, 66-7; **1**(3), 1970, 6-9; **1**(4), 1970, 6-9.

Frodsham

THORNELEY, S., ed. *Frodsham parish church (St. Lawrence) registers: baptisms 1558 to 1812.* Worcester: Ebenr. Baylis & Son, 1913. Includes list of parish records.

THORNELEY, S., ed. *Frodsham parish church (St. Lawrence) registers: burials 1558 to 1812.* Worcester: Ebenr. Baylis & Son, 1912.

THORNELEY, S., ed. *Frodsham parish church (St. Lawrence) registers: marriages, 1558 to 1812.* Chester: Courant Press. 1908.

Gawsworth

DICKINSON, ROBERT, ed. *The registers of the parish church of Gawsworth in the County of Chester, 1557-1837.* Ancient Monuments Society, 1955.

POLEHAMPTON, H.E. ed. 'Marriages at Gawsworth, 1557 to 1812', in PHILLIMORE, W.P.W., & CHOICE, LEOPOLD, eds. *C.P.R.M.* **1**. *P.P.R.S.* 111. Phillimore & Co., 1909, 119-52.

Guilden Sutton

S., E. 'Parish register of Guilden Sutton, 1595-1726', *C.Sf.* 4th series 1, 1966, 34-41. Transcript.

Hatherlow

AXON, GEOFFREY R. 'Hatherlow Chapel baptismal register, 1732-1781', *L.C.A.S.* 44, 1927, 56-99. Full transcript.

'Hatherlow Chapel baptismal record, 1732-1781', *South Cheshire Family History Society quarterly journal* 4, 1991, 12-13.

Heswall

MAY, THOMAS HENRY. *The registers of baptisms, marriages and burials in the parish of Heswall, in the County and Diocese of Chester, from their commencement to the year 1729, together with a table of the rectors of Heswall from the year 1300 to the present time, and a terrier of lands, fees, charges etc., in the year 1733.* Guildford: Billing and Sons, [1897?]

Knutsford

GAUTREY, A.J. 'Misplaced persons: Knutsford parish registers, marriages 1693-1812', *N.C.F.H.* 6(2), 1979, 58-9. Strays only.

Lymm

HATTON, F., & INNES, MISS. 'Marriages at Lymm 1568 to 1812', in PHILLIMORE, W.P.W., & CHOICE, LEOPOLD, eds. *C.P.R.M.* 1. *P.P.R.S.* 111. Phillimore & Co., 1909, 59-97.

MORRIS, DAVID, & MORRIS, HILARY. 'The Lymm parish registers', in *Lymm and District Local History Society.* Lymm: G.H.Thomas, 1972, 60-62. Reprinted from the Society's *newsletter.* General discussion of their potential for historical research.

JACKSON, MICHAEL. 'Lymm strays', *J.L.D.L.H.S.* 2(1), 1986, 10-12. Baptisms and marriages of Lymm people in Lancashire parish registers.

JACKSON, MICHAEL. 'Lymm Primitive Methodist chapel, Eagle Brow: register of baptisms, 1837-1862', *Q.J.L.D.* 6(2), 1983, 11-23; 66(3), 1983, 1-10. Transcript.

'Wesleyan Methodist Chapel, Lymm: register, 1809-1837', *F.H.S.C.J.* 8(3), 1979, 20-21. Baptisms.

Macclesfield

'Cheshire strays', *F.H.S.C.J.* 6(2), 1977, 9.

Extracts from Macclesfield St. Michael parish register, 1725-1894.

Marple

CHOICE, LEOPOLD, ed. 'Marriages at Marple, 1656 to 1754', in PHILLIMORE, W.P.W., & CHOICE, LEOPOLD, eds. *C.P.R.M.* 1. *P.P.R.S.* 111. Phillimore & Co., 1909, 11-29.

Marton

CHOICE, LEOPOLD, ed. 'Marriages at Marton, 1563 to 1769', in his *C.P.R.M.* 5. *P.P.R.S.* 216. Phillimore, 1914, 81-92.

CHOICE, LEOPOLD, ed. 'Marton marriages: addenda et corrigenda', in his *C.P.R.M.* 5. *P.P.R.S.* 216. Phillimore, 1914, 119-22.

Middlewich

'Marriage licenses, Middlewich, 1808-1837', *F.H.S.C.J.* 1(2), 1970, 3. Lists 18 licenses, mainly 1808-10.

Nantwich

CHURCH, CONSTANCE. 'Untimely deaths at Nantwich in the 17th century', *F.H.S.C.J.* 9(4), 1980, 5-8. Extracts from the parish register.

Norbury

See Poynton

Northwich

FROBISHER, K.A. *A century stand: the story of Emmanuel Evangelist Church, Northwich, 1882-1982.* Northwich: [ ], 1982. Appendices include marriages, 1910-79, and baptisms, 1929-78.

See also Dane Bridge

Overchurch

'The parish register of Overchurch in Wirral', *C.Sf.* 3rd series 6, 1907, 87. Transcript of the bishop's transcript for 1619, recently discovered.

Over Peover

CARR, PHILIP H. 'Strays at Over Peover, 1853-1956', *F.H.S.C.J.* 7(2), 1978, 13-14; 7(4), 1978, 14-15; 8(1), 1978, 14-16; 8(2), 1979, 17-18; 8(3), 1979, 19; 8(4), 1979, 25. From the parish register.

Pott Shrigley

CHOICE, L., ed. 'Marriages at Pott Shrigley, 1685 to 1751', in his *C.P.R.M.* **5.** *P.P.R.S.* **216.** Phillimore, 1914, 107-11.

Poynton

SHERCLIFF, W.H. 'The parish registers of Poynton and Norbury chapels', *Poynton Local History Society newsletter* **5**, 1982, 9-16. Analytical discussion.

CHOICE, LEOPOLD, ed. 'Marriages at Poynton-cum-Worth 1723 to 1753', in his *C.P.R.M.* **5.** *P.P.R.S.* **216.** Phillimore, 1914, 93-9.

Prestbury

CHOICE, JAMES, ed. *The register book of christenings, weddings and burials within the parish of Prestbury in the County of Chester, 1560-1636.* L.C.R.S. **5**, 1881.

CHOICE, LEOPOLD, ed. *Marriages at Prestbury, 1637 to 1812.* C.P.R.M. **2-4.** P.P.R.S. **137, 161 & 182.** Phillimore & Co., 1910-12.

SANT, TONY. 'An assortment of untimely ends from Prestbury parish registers', *N.C.F.H.* **18**(1), 1991, 10. Brief list of burials.

HARTLEY, B. 'Prestbury parish registers', *F.H.S.C.J.* **20**(3), 1991, 23-5. Includes a list of the townships in one of Cheshire's largest parishes, and of the parishes formed out of it, 19th c.

Rostherne

SANT, A.J. 'Mistakes from Rostherne parish registers', *N.C.F.H.* **13**(2), 1986, 58. Brief note.

Shocklach

B[ENNETT] J.H.E. 'Extracts from Shocklach parish register', *C.Sf.* 3rd series **18**, 1923, 55-6, *passim*. Brief extract, 16-17th c.

Siddington

CHOICE, LEOPOLD, ed. 'Marriages at Siddington, 1722 to 1783', in his *C.P.R.M.* **5.** *P.P.R.S.* **216.** Phillimore, 1914, 101-5.

Stockport

BULKELEY, E.W., [ed.] *The parish registers of Saint Mary, Stockport, containing the baptisms, marriages and burials from 1584-1620, with notes.* Stockport: Swain & Co., 1889. See also *C.N.Q.* **6-9**, 1886-9, *passim*.

WILD, W.I. 'Stockport parish church register', *C.N.Q.* N.S., **2**, 1897, 31-9, 75-101 & 179-85. Covers 1619-27.

HOPWOOD, JOHN, et al. *Stockport marriages 1799-1837.* 3 microfiche. Manchester: Manchester & Lancashire Family History Society, 1988. Alphabetical index.

McKENNA, S. 'Notes on Mount Tabor, Stockport, baptism register', *N.C.F.H.* **8**(1), 1981, 17-18. Brief note on discrepancies in the 19th c. register.

Tattenhall

'Tattenhall parish register: baptisms 1812-1835: index of surnames appearing', *F.H.S.C.J.* **3**(3), 1972, 13-14; **7**(1), 1977, 15-16; **7**(2), 1978, 17.

'Marriage licenses in Cheshire, 1806-1900', *F.H.S.C.J.,* **2**, 1971, 14; **2**(3), 1971, 14. Filed with Tattenhall parish records.

Taxal

CHOICE, LEOPOLD, ed. 'Marriages at Taxal, 1611-1812', in PHILLIMORE, W.P.W., & CHOICE, LEOPOLD, eds. *C.P.R.M.* **1.** *P.P.R.S.* **111.** Phillimore & Co., 1909, 31-58.

CHOICE, LEOPOLD, ed. 'Appendix: Marriages at Taxal, 1813 to 1837', in his *C.P.R.M.* **5.** *P.P.R.S.* **216.** Phillimore, 1914, 113-8.

Upton

IRVINE, WM. FERGUSSON, ed. *The registers of Upton in Overchurch, Cheshire, 1660-1812.* Parish Register Society **33.** 1900. Includes biographical notes on incumbents.

Wallasey

HANCE, EDWARD M., & MORTON, T.N. 'Extracts from the registers of the parish church of St. Hilary, Wallasey, with notes thereupon', *H.S.L.C.* **35**, 1883, 37-128. Not a full transcript, but includes much miscellaneous information, e.g. pedigree of Coventry family, in addition to births, marriages and deaths.

Warburton

'Marriages at Warburton church of men from outside the county', *F.H.S.C.J.* **2**(4), 1971, 11.

Weaverham

BEBBINGTON, CHARLES E. 'The parish church of Weaverham and its registers', *L.C.A.S.* **54**, 1939, 209-46. Includes a brief discussion of the registers; also list of vicars, 13-20th c. extracts from churchwardens' accounts, list of papers, *etc.*

Wilmslow

PEEL, ROBERT. 'Some notes on Wilmslow parish registers', *L.C.A.S.* **33**, 1915, 161-77. General discussion; few extracts.

Witton

MUSGRAVE, KEITH & MOILLIET, ANDREW. *Surname index and extracts from the registers of St. Helens church, Witton, January 1754 to February 1792.* [Northwich]: F.H.S.C., Northwich Group, 1986.

MUSGRAVE, KEITH & MOILLIET, ANDREW. *Surnames index and extracts from the marriage registers of St. Helen's church, Witton (February 1792 to December 1851).* [ ]: [F.H.S.C?], 1986.

MUSGRAVE, KEITH & MOILLIET, ANDREW. *Surname index from the baptism registers of St. Helens church, Witton (January 1813 to December 1851).* [Northwich]: F.H.S.C., Northwich Group, 1987.

6. MONUMENTAL INSCRIPTIONS

A. *General*

Monumental inscriptions frequently include much more information than is provided in the parish register, and are of considerable value. Many have been transcribed and published; for an extensive listing of these (which is much more comprehensive than can be attempted here) see:

BEAZLEY, F.C., ed. *Calendar of persons commemorated in monumental inscriptions, and of abstracts of wills, administrations, etc., contained in books relating to Lancashire and Cheshire.* L.C.R.S. **76**. 1922. Index to monumental inscriptions and wills in 162 printed works (which are listed).

For an up to date listing of manuscript monumental inscription transcripts, reference should be made to Langston's book cited at the beginning of section 5. Lists of churchyards whose memorials have been recorded are given in:

'Memorial inscriptions index', *N.C.F.H.* **20**(2), 1993, 56-7.

'North and East Cheshire churchyards whose monumental inscriptions are known to have been recorded', *N.C.F.H.* **7**(2), 1980, 52-3. See also **7**(3), 1980, 64.

For manuscript transcripts of Cheshire monumental inscriptions held at Manchester Central Library, see:

MOILLIET, ANDREW. 'The Owen manuscript collection', *F.H.S.C.J.* **15**(3), 1986, 10-11.

There are a number of general works including monumental inscriptions:

GLYNNE, SIR STEPHEN R. *Notes on the churches of Cheshire.* ed. J.A. Atkinson, Cm.S., N.S., **32**. 1894. Includes some inscriptions.

B[EAZLEY], F.C. 'Corrigenda to monumental inscriptions in Helsby's Ormerod's *Cheshire: Hundred of Wirral', C.Sf.* 3rd series **7**, 1910, 80-81, 84, 86, 88, 90, & 91-2.

S[TEWART]-B[ROWN], R. 'Monumental inscriptions to Cheshire folk, 1600-1718', *C.Sf.* 3rd series **14**, 1919, 4-5. From Le Neve's *Monumenta Anglicana.*

'Monumental inscriptions of Cheshire folk in other counties', *C.Sf.* 3rd series **8**, 1911, *passim.*

LONGBOTTOM, F.W. *Church heraldry in the Diocese of Chester: a personal survey.* Childer Thornton: the author, 1988- . v.1. Rural Deanery of Wirral South. No more published. Includes pedigrees of Stanley of Hooton and Banbury of Stanney.

Effigies, brasses and hatchments have all been the subjects of works of potential genealogical value:

BLAIR, C. 'The pre-Reformation effigies of Cheshire', *L.C.A.S.* **60**, 1948, 117-47; **61**, 1949, 91-120. Primarily from an artistic point of view.

CROSSLEY, FRED. H. 'The post-Reformation effigies and monuments of Cheshire (1550-1800)', *H.S.L.C.* **91**, 1939, 1-123. List with descriptions.

ANGUS-BUTTERWORTH, L.M. 'The monumental brasses of Cheshire', *L.C.A.S.* **55**, 1940, 81-106. Brief.

THORNLEY, J.L. *Monumental brasses of Lancashire and Cheshire, with some account of the persons represented.* Hull: William Andrews & Co., London: Simpkin Marshall & Co., 1893.

WALLER, J.G. 'On certain church brasses in Cheshire and Lancashire', *Journal of the British Archaeological Association* **5**, 1850, 256-65.

CHRISTOPHER, M.G. 'Five Cheshire brasses', *Transactions of the Monumental Brass Society* **10**(2), 1964, 56-7. Brief notes.

SUMMERS, PETER, & TITTERTON, JOHN. *Hatchments in Britain, 8: Cheshire, Derbyshire, Leicestershire, Lincolnshire Nottinghamshire and Staffordshire.* Chichester: Phillimore & Co., 1988.

B. *Local*

Acton
HALL, JAMES. 'Church monuments in Acton Church', *C.Sf.* 3rd series **1**, 1896, 76-8.

Alderley
WAY, D.H., et al. *The gravestone inscriptions of St. Mary's church, Alderley, Cheshire.* [Monumental inscriptions] 17. N.C.F.H.S., [1985/6?]

Antrobus
NOBLE, VACKY. *A transcript of the monumental inscriptions and churchwarden's accounts, St. Mark's Church, Antrobus, Cheshire.* [ ]: F.H.S.C., 1992.

Appleton Thorn
NOBLE, VACKY. *A transcript of the monumental inscriptions of St. Cross church, Appleton Thorn, Cheshire.* 1 fiche [ ]: F.H.S.C., 1992.

FOWLER, L.E. 'A Cheshire village at war: a commentary on the Appleton Thorn war memorial', *Cheshire history* **27**, 1991, 15-19. Includes biographical notes on persons commemorated, 1914-18.

Ashton on Mersey
SHEPHERD, P. 'Monumental inscriptions from St. Martin's parish church, Ashton-on-Mersey, Cheshire', *Manchester genealogist,* **4**(2), 1968, 6-7; **4**(3), 1968, 10-13; **4**(4), 1968, 16; **5**(4), 1969, 24-5

Astbury
The memorial inscriptions of St. Mary's churchyard, Astbury. 4 fiche. Congleton: F.H.S.C., Congleton Group, 1990.

Audlem
'Monumental inscriptions at Audlem', *C.Sf.* 3rd series **29**, 1935, 78.

Backford
See Stoak.

Baddiley
HALL, JAMES. 'Church monuments, iv: Baddiley church', *C.Sf.* 3rd series **4**, 1904, 70-71.

Barnston
Record of monumental inscriptions at Christ's Church, Barnston, Wirral. 2 fiche. [ ]: F.H.S.C., 1985.

Barnton
A transcript of the monumental inscriptions of Christchurch, Barnton, Cheshire. 2 fiche. [ ]: F.H.S.C., 1992.

Barthomley

BULLOUGH, HERBERT. *St. Bertoline, Barthomley, Cheshire: monumental inscriptions.* 1 fiche. [ ]: F.H.S.C., 1992.

Bebbington

See Chester. Holy Trinity

Bidston

IRVINE, Wm. FERGUSSON. 'Monumental inscriptions in Bidston church', *C.Sf.* 3rd series **3**, 1901, 117.
See also Woodchurch.

Bollington

BRIGG, TOM, et al. *The parish church of St. John the Baptist Bollington.* 3 fiche. [Monumental inscriptions] **22**. N.C.F.H.S., 1987.
See also Wilmslow

Bosley

MACCLESFIELD FERRETS. *Memorial inscriptions in the churchyard of Bosley St. Marys, nr. Macclesfield, Cheshire.* 1 fiche. [Monumental inscriptions] **6**. N.C.F.H.S., 1987.

Bramhall Hall

R[YLANDS], J.P. 'A memorial stained glass at Bramhall Hall, near Stockport', *C.Sf.* 3rd series **9**, 1913, 14.

Bromborough

B[EAZLEY], F.C. Monumental inscriptions at Bromborough', *C.Sf.* 3rd series **27**, 1934, 25-45, *passim.*
FOXCROFT, JACK, FOXCROFT, DOREEN, & TWEEDDALE, PETER. *A record of the inscriptions on memorials erected in the churchyard and interior of St. Barnabas parish church, Bromborough.* 2 fiche. [ ]: F.H.S.C., 1988.

Bunbury

RYLANDS, J. PAUL, & BEAZLEY, F.C. *The monuments at Bunbury church, Cheshire.* Privately printed, 1918. Expanded from:
RYLANDS, J. PAUL, & BEAZLEY, F.C. 'The monuments at Bunbury church, Cheshire', *H.S.L.C.* **69**; N.S., **33**, 1917, 97-145; **70**; N.S., **34**, 1918, 72-131. Includes pedigrees of Broster of Chester, 17th c., and Gardner of Southley and Tilston Fearnall, 17-18th c.

Capenhurst

FOXCROFT, JACK. *A record of the inscriptions on memorials erected in the churchyard and interior of Holy Trinity parish church, Capenhurst.* [ ]: F.H.S.C., 1990.

Cheadle Hulme

CLARKE, A.G., *et al. The monumental inscriptions of All Saints church, Cheadle Hulme.* [Monumental inscriptions] **25**. N.C.F.H.S., 1993.

Chester

'Monumental inscriptions from the churches and burial ground cleared for the inner ring road or for development', *J.C.A.H.S.* **51**, 1964, 55-76. Chester inscriptions.

Holy Trinity

'Randle Holmes's notes on Cheshire churches', *C.Sf.* 3rd series **3**, 1901, 17-19. 17th c. heraldic notes on Holy Trinity, Chester, Bebbington, and Eastham in Wirral.

St. Bridget

BENNETT, J.H.E. 'Arms and inscriptions sometime in the church of St. Bridget, Chester', *J.C.A.H.S.* N.S., **23**, 1918-19, 10-37.

St. Mary on the Hill

S., A.G. 'Memorials to soldiers, etc., at St. Mary on the Hill, Chester', *C.Sf.* 3rd series **36**, 1948, 4.

St. Michael

B[ENNETT], J.H.E. 'Monumental inscriptions in St. Michael's church, Chester', *C.Sf.* 3rd series **30**, 1935, 78-97, *passim.*

Cholmondeley

B[ENNETT], J.H.E. 'Arms in Cholmondeley chapel', *C.Sf.* 3rd series **17**, 1922, 35.

Church Lawton

NUNN, H. 'Lawton', *A.N.Q.* **4**, 1884, 10-11. See also 16. Monumental inscriptions.

Church Minshull

B[ENNETT], J.H.E. Monumental inscriptions *etc.*, at Church Minshull', *C.Sf.* 3rd series **32**, 1938, 89-113, *passim.*
R[YLANDS], J.P. 'Heraldic glass at Church Minshull in 1572', *C.Sf.* 3rd series **14**, 1919, 71-2, 73, 75, 76-7 & 78.

Congleton

BINGHAM, PHYLLIS V. *The memorial inscriptions and pew records of St. Peter's church, Congleton, Cheshire.* 1 fiche. [ ]: F.H.S.C., [198-?] Includes pew lists of 1766 and 1840.

Crowton

BULLOCK, MICHAEL R. *A transcript of the monumental inscriptions of Christ Church, Crowton, Cheshire.* 1 fiche. [ ]: F.H.S.C., 1992.

Daresbury

DIBBLE, S., & NOBLE, V. *A transcript of the monumental inscriptions of the new graveyard at All Saints, Daresbury, Cheshire.* 1 fiche. [F.H.S.C], 1992.

R[YLANDS], J.P. 'Notes taken at Daresbury church in 1572 and about 1670', *C.Sf.* 3rd series 9 1913, 45-6.

'All Saints, Daresbury', *F.H.S.C.J.* 7(1) 1977, 12. Index to surnames in part of the graveyard.

Disley

DISLEY LOCAL HISTORY SOCIETY. *Graveyard survey: St. Marys parish church.* Disley: the Society, 1994.

Eastham

B[EAZLEY], F.C. 'Monumental inscriptions at Eastham', *C.Sf.* 3rd series 10, 1914, *passim.* *See also* Chester. Holy Trinity.

Effwood Hall

APPLEBY, J.E. 'Monumental inscriptions of the private burial ground of Effwood Hall, in the Goyt Valley, Cheshire; the Hall now being demolished, but the burial ground being still in existence', *F.H.S.C.J.* 8(4), 1979, 22.

Farndon

BRATT, C. 'A few strays from Farndon churchyard', *F.H.S.C.J.* 8(1), 1978, 28.

Frodsham

R[YLANDS], J.P. 'Armorial bearings in Frodsham church in 1591', *C.Sf.* 3rd series 13, 1918, 96.

Gawsworth

CLARKE, WILLIAM EDGAR. 'The Gawsworth armorials', *Transactions of the Ancient Monuments Society* N.S., 3, 1957, 63-78.

SANDERS, COLIN & SANDERS, JUDY. *The monumental inscriptions of St. James, Gawsworth.* 2 fiche. [Monumental inscriptions] 19. N.C:F.H.S, [1977/8]

Grappenhall

R[YLANDS], J.P. 'Some monumental inscriptions in Grappenhall church yard', *C.Sf.* 3rd series 13, 1918, 68-9, 71, 73-4, 78, 81 & 84.

Great Budworth

HOOLE, JOHN. 'Inscriptions on churches in Cheshire', *C.Sf.* 3rd series 28, 1935, 52-3. Monumental inscriptions from Great Budworth and Mobberley.

The parish church of St. Mary and All Saints, Great Budworth, Cheshire. 5 fiche. [Monumental inscriptions] 15. N.C.F.H.S., [199-?]

Great Warford

Great Warford Baptist Chapel, Cheshire: monumental inscriptions. 1 fiche. [ ]: F.H.S.C., 1992.

Guilden Sutton

A transcript of the monumental inscriptions of St. Johns church, Guilden Sutton, and All Saints church, Hoole, Cheshire (including Guilden Sutton Methodist Chapel, and Hoole public war memorial). 1 fiche. [ ]: F.H.S.C., 1993.

Handley

B[ENNETT], J.H.E. 'Inscriptions *etc.,* at Handley church', *C.Sf.* 3rd series 30, 1935, 25-6.

Hargrave

A transcript of the monumental inscriptions of St. Peter's, Hargrave, Cheshire. 1 fiche. [ ]: F.H.S.C., 1993.

Hartford

BULLOCK, MICHAEL R. *A transcript of the monumental inscriptions of St. John the Baptist, Hartford, Cheshire.* 2 fiche. [ ]: F.H.S.C., 1992.

Harthill

MATHEWS, GODFREY W. 'Notes on the parish and church of Harthill', *H.S.L.C.* 81, 1929, 38-50. Includes some inscriptions.

Heaton Norris
Heaton Norris Christ Church M.I. with grave plan. 4 fiche. [Monumental inscriptions] 18. N.C.F.H.S., [199-?].

LITTON, PAULINE. 'Christ Church, Heaton Norris', *N.C.F.H.* 4(4), 1977, 100-104. Discussion of monumental inscriptions.

Henbury
Memorial inscriptions in the churchyard of Henbury St. Thomas, nr. Macclesfield, Cheshire. [ ]: F.H.S.C., 1989.

High Leigh
RYLANDS, J.P. 'Armorial glass in the chapel at High Leigh', *C.Sf.* 3rd series **13**, 1918, 35-6.

Higher Bebington
Monumental inscriptions of Christ Church, Higher Bebington. 2 fiche. [ ]: F.H.S.C., 1982.

Hoole
See Guilden Sutton.

Huxley
JONES, HARTLEY. *A transcript of the monumental inscriptions of Huxley Methodist Church burial ground, Cheshire.* 1 fiche. F.H.S.C., 1992.

Ince
SLATER, F.G. 'Some early 18th century brasses in Ince church', *J.C.A.H.S.* N.S., **1**, 1909, 36-53.

Knutsford
NORTH CHESHIRE FAMILY HISTORY SOCIETY. *The St. Cross, Knutsford, monumental inscriptions.* [Monumental inscriptions] 11. N.C.F.H.S. 1975.

NORTH CHESHIRE FAMILY HISTORY SOCIETY. *The parish church of St. John the Baptist, Knutsford, Cheshire: monumental inscriptions.* 3 fiche. [Monumental inscriptions] 23 N.C.F.H.S., [199-?]

Lindow
CLARKE, ALAN, et al. *The monumental inscriptions of St. John the Evangelist, Lindow, Wilmslow.* 2 fiche. [Monumental inscriptions] **8**, N.C.F.H.S., 1991.

Little Leigh
A transcript of the monumental inscriptions of St. Michael's church, Little Leigh, and All Saints church, Lach Dennis, Cheshire. 1 fiche. [ ]: F.H.S.C., 1992.

Lostock Gralam
BULLOCK, MICHAEL R. *A transcript of the monumental inscriptions of St. John the Evangelist, Lostock Gralam, Cheshire.* 3 fiche. [ ]: F.H.S.C., 1992.

Low Marple
CLARKE, A.G. *Monumental inscriptions of St. Martins church, Low Marple, Cheshire.* [Monumental inscriptions] **28**. 1 fiche. N.C.F.H.S., 1993.

Lower Peover
NORTH CHESHIRE FAMILY HISTORY SOCIETY. *Monumental inscriptions of St. Oswalds church, Lower Peover, Cheshire.* 2 fiche. [Monumental inscriptions] **20**. N.C.F.H.S., 1975.

Lymm
The monumental inscriptions of St. Mary's parish church, Lymm, c. 1630-1990. [Lymm]: Lymm & District Local History Society, 1990.

RYLANDS, J. PAUL. *The shields of arms formerly in the windows of the parish church of Lymm, Co. Chester, as illustrative of the origin of several local coats of arms.* Liverpool: T.Brakell, 1879.

RYLANDS, J. PAUL. 'The shields of arms formerly in the windows of the parish church of Lymm, County Chester, as illustrative of the origin of several local coats of arms', *H.S.L.C.* **31**; 3rd series **7**, 1879, 1-12.

Macclesfield
Christchurch
DEWDNEY, PETER. *A transcript of the monumental inscriptions, Christ Church, Macclesfield, Cheshire.* 2 fiche. [ ]: F.H.S.C., 1992.

DEWDNEY, PETER. 'Stones behind the stones: the Methodist Saints gravestone in the churchyard of Christ Church, Macclesfield', *F.H.S.C.J.* **22**(3) 1993, 23-4.

'Christ Church, Macclesfield', *Lancashire and Cheshire historian* **1**, 1965, 157-8. Surnames from monumental inscriptions.

St. Michael
WAY, DEREK H., *et al. Memorial inscriptions of St. Michaels church Macclesfield, Cheshire.* 1 fiche. [Monumental inscriptions] **3**. N.C.F.H.S., 1987.

St. Paul
MACCLESFIELD FERRETS. *Memorial inscriptions in the churchyard of St. Paul's, Macclesfield, Cheshire.* [Monumental inscriptions] **9**. 1 fiche. N.C.F.H.S., 1989.

Macclesfield Forest
Graveyard inscriptions of Forest Chapel, Macclesfield, recorded in the summer, 1981. 1 fiche. [Monumental inscriptions] **2**. N.C.F.H.S., 1982.

Marbury
HALL, JAMES. 'Church monuments iii: Marbury church', *C.Sf.* 3rd series **2** 1895, 9-11.

Marston
A transcript of the monumental inscriptions of St. Paul's church, Marston, Cheshire. [ ]: F.H.S.C., 1993.

Marton
MARTON & DISTRICT PRIMARY SCHOOL. *The monumental inscriptions of St. James & St. Paul [Marton].* 2 fiche. [Monumental inscriptions] **5**. N.C.F.H.S., 1984.

Mickle Trafford
JONES, HARTLEY. *A transcript of the monumental inscriptions of Mickle Trafford Methodist burial ground, Cheshire.* 1 fiche. [ ]. F.H.S.C., 1993.

Mobberley
DAY, H., & CLARKE, A.G., et al. *Monumental inscriptions of St. Wilfred's church, Mobberley.* 3 fiche. [Monumental inscriptions] **24**. N.C.F.H.S., 1993.
'Some curious epitaphs at Mobberley', *C.Sf.* 3rd series **11**, 1915, 3-4. Includes will of Francis Hulme, 1659.
See also Great Budworth.

Nantwich
Barony All Saints, Nantwich, Cheshire: monumental inscriptions. 2 fiche. [ ]: F.H.S.C., 1992.

Newbold Astbury
B[ENNETT], J.H.E. Monumental inscriptions *etc.*, of Newbold Astbury', *C.Sf.* 3rd series **31**, 1937, 101-7, *passim.*

Norley
BULLOCK, MICHAEL R. *A transcript of the monumental inscriptions of St. John's church, Norley, Cheshire.* 2 fiche. [ ]: F.H.S.C., 1993.

Northenden
St. Wilfred's church, Northenden, Diocese of Manchester: monumental inscriptions. 4 fiche. [ ]: F.H.S.C., 1992.

Over
'St Chad's. Over, near Winsford', *F.H.S.C.J.* **6**(4) 1977, 18-19. Index of surnames on gravestones.

Overchurch
See Woodchurch.

Over Knutsford
BETHELL, D. 'Over Knutsford monumental inscriptions', *Lancashire and Cheshire historian* **1**, 1965, 81-2, 107-8 & 129-30.

Over Peover
The monumental inscriptions, St. Lawrence, Over Peover churchyard, Cheshire. 2 fiche. [Monumental inscriptions] **16**. N.C.F.H.S., 1972.
See also Snelson.

Plemstall
B[EAZLEY], F.C. 'Monumental inscriptions in Plemstall church', *C.Sf.* 3rd series **10**, 1914, 24-39, *passim.*

Pott Shrigley
WAY, DEREK. et al. *Gravestone inscriptions of St. Christophers church, Pott Shrigley, Cheshire.* 1 fiche. [Monumental inscriptions] **7**. N.C.F.H.S., 1983.

Poynton

NORTH CHESHIRE FAMILY HISTORY SOCIETY. *The parish church of St. George, Poynton, Cheshire: the monumental inscriptions.* 3 fiche. [Monumental inscriptions] 1. N.C.F.H.S., [198-?]

Rainow

WAY, DEREK, et al. *Gravestone inscriptions of Rainow Church of England, Cheshire, together with the Pleasance graveyard.* 1 fiche. [Monumental inscriptions] 4. N.C.F.H.S., 1983.
Gravestone inscriptions of Rainow Methodist Chapel. 1 fiche. [Monumental inscriptions] 12. N.C.F.H.S., 1981.

Ringway

HALL, LESLEY W., & PILGRIM, PETER J. *Monumental inscriptions of St. Mary's Ringway (church now disused).* [ ]: F.H.S.C., 1988.

Rostherne

NORTH CHESHIRE FAMILY HISTORY SOCIETY. *Monumental inscriptions of St. Mary's church, Rostherne, Cheshire.* 4 fiche. Monumental inscriptions 14. N.C.F.H.S., [198-?]
See also Wilmslow

Siddington

GRAVEYARD FERRETS. *Memorial inscriptions in the churchyard of All Saints, Siddington, Cheshire.* 1 fiche. [Monumental inscriptions] 10. N.C.F.H.S., 1987.

Snelson

Snelson and Over Peover Methodist chapel, Cheshire: monumental inscriptions. 1 fiche. [ ]. F.H.S.C., 1992.

Spital Boughton

JONES, HARTLEY, & SHEPHERD, CHRISTOPHER. *A transcript of the monumental inscriptions of St. Giles Cemetery, Spital Boughton, Chester.* 1 fiche. [ ]. F.H.S.C., 1992.

Spurstow Hall

B[ENNETT], J.H.E. 'Arms in Spurstow Hall', *C.Sf.* 3rd series 16, 1921, 42-4.

Stoak

RYLANDS, J.PAUL, & BEAZLEY, F.C. *The monumental and other inscriptions in the churches of Stoak, Backford and Thornton-le-Moors, in the County of Chester, copied in the year 1904 and annotated.* [ ], 1905. Reprinted from *H.S.L.C.* 57; N.S., 21, 1905, 120-207. Includes folded pedigree of Bunbury, 17-18th c.

Stockton Heath

A transcript of the monumental inscriptions of St. Thomas parish church, Stockton Heath, Cheshire. 3 fiche. [ ]. F.H.S.C., 1992.

Stretton

'Armorial glass at Stretton chapel in Bucklow Hundred', *C.Sf.* 3rd series 13, 1918, 39-40.

Sutton

WAY, D.H., et al. *Memorial inscriptions in the churchyard of Sutton St. James, nr. Macclesfield, Cheshire.* 2 fiche. [Monumental inscriptions] 13. N.C.F.H.S., 1987.

Tarvin

'Surnames appearing on the tombstones in Tarvin churchyard', *F.H.S.C.J.* 3(2), 1972, 4 & 9.

Thornton le Moors

See Stoak

Thurstaston

See Woodchurch

Tilstone Fearnall

St. Jude's church, Tilstone Fearnall, Cheshire: monumental inscriptions. [ ]: F.H.S.C., 1992.

Upton Hall

See Woodchurch

Wallasey

LANGLEY, C.E. 'Headstones at Friends (Quaker) Meeting House, Withers Lane, Wallasey', *F.H.S.C.J.* 12(1), 1982, 13-15.

Walton

NOBLE, VACKY. *A transcript of the monumental inscriptions of St. John the Evangelist, Walton, Cheshire.* 1 fiche. [ ]: F.H.S.C., 1992.

Waverton

BEAZLEY, F.C. 'Monumental inscriptions at Waverton', *C.Sf.* 3rd series **20**, 1924, 67-8 & 70.

JEFFREYS, G. ALAN. *An abstract of the monumental inscriptions of the parish church of St. Peter, Waverton.* 1 fiche. [ ]: F.H.S.C., 1993.

Weaverham

TARRANT, H. *Monumental inscriptions of St. Mary the Virgin, Weaverham, Cheshire.* 2 fiche. [Monumental inscriptions] **26.** [ ]: N.C.F.H.S., 1980.

Willaston

B[EAZLEY], F.C. 'Monumental inscriptions at Willaston in Wirral', *C.Sf.* 3rd series **22**, 1927, 44, 45, & 82-3.

Wilmslow

NICHOLSON, J. HOLME. 'Wilmslow church and its monuments', *L.C.A.S.* **8**, 1890, 53-62.

CLARKE, ALAN & CLARKE, RHODA. *Monumental inscriptions of Quaker burial ground, Water Lane, Wilmslow, Cheshire.* 1 fiche. [Monumental inscriptions] **26.** [ ]: N.C.F.H.S., 1989. This fiche also includes: DAY, HARRY. *Monumental inscriptions of St. James Church, Woodhead,* and DAY, H. *Monumental inscriptions of Holy Trinity church, Rostherne with Bollington, Cheshire.*
'Dean Row Dissenters' Chapel, Wilmslow: monumental inscriptions', *F.H.S.C.J.* 6(3), 1977, 10-12.

Wirral

BEAZLEY, F.C. 'Wirral records of the XVll century', *H.S.L.C.* **77**, N.S., **41**, 1925, 76-152. Pt.1. Church notes from Harl. ms. 2151. (Includes monumental inscriptions). Pt.2. Inscriptions before 1700, taken by J. Paul Rylands and F.C. Beazley. Pt.3. The visitation of Cheshire, 1663-4, by William Dugdale, esq., Norroy. See also **78**; N.S., **42**, 144 for further inscriptions.

Woodchurch

GENEALOGIST. 'Randle Holmes's notes on Cheshire churches', *C.Sf.* 3rd series **3**, 1901, 28-9. 17th c. heraldic notes on Woodchurch in Wirral, Overchurch, Bidston, Thurstaston, and Upton Hall.

Woodford

CLARKE, A.G. *The monumental inscriptions of Christ Church, Woodford.* 3 fiche. [Monumental inscriptions] **27.** N.C.F.H.S., 1993.

Woodhead

See Wilmslow

Wrenbury

'Church monuments, II: Wrenbury church', *C.Sf.* 3rd series **1**, 1896, 79. See also **2**, 1896, 9.

Wybunbury

B[ENNETT]. J.H.E. 'Some monumental etc inscriptions at Wybunbury', *C.Sf.* 3rd series **32**, 1938, 41-65, *passim.*

C. *Family*

Alsager

HOUGHTON, B.T. 'Monumental inscriptions to Cheshire folk in Staffordshire churches: Standon', *C.Sf.* 3rd series **22**, 1927, 44-5. Memorial to Samuel Alsager, 1707.

Baggalegh

CROSTON, JAMES. 'Monumental effigy at Baguley Hall', *L.C.A.S.* **4**, 1886, 149-54. Of Sir William Baggalegh, 14th c.

Barker

'The Barker family of Chester', *C.Sf.* 3rd series **23**, 1928, 81 & 83-4. Monumental inscriptions at Chester.

Becket

B[ENNETT], J.H.E. 'Becket memorials in Brereton church', *C.Sf.* 3rd series **45**, 1951, 58.

Bennett

B[ENNETT], J.H.E. 'The story of a misleading monument in Holy Trinity church, Chester', *Cheshire sheaf* 3rd series **34**, 1941, 57-9. Bennett family 17th c.

Boydell

PHELPS. J.J. 'The Boydell effigy at Grappenhall', *L.C.A.S.* **44**, 1927, 8-16. See also **47**, 1930-31, 139-54. Medieval.

Bramfield
See Jenks

Bulkeley
'A Bulkeley monument at St. Johns, Chester', *C.Sf.* 3rd series **28**, 1935, 5-6. 17th c.

Burganey
'Burganey family of Pulford', *C.Sf.* 3rd series **29**, 1935, 54. Monumental inscriptions, 18-19th c.

Calveley
BLAIR, C. *The effigy and tomb of Sir Hugh Calveley (Bunbury church, Cheshire).* Bunbury papers **4**. Bunbury: M.H. Ridgway, 1951. 1394.

Corbet
See Tollemache

Corles
'Corles family of Chester', *C.Sf.* 3rd series **19**, 1924, 75. Inscriptions at Worcester, mid-19th c.

Cotes
B[ENNETT], J.H.E. 'Cotes monument', *C.Sf.* 3rd series **10**, 1914, 57-8. 17th c. monument at St. Johns, Chester.

Cottingham
See Glegg

Cragg
VIATOR. 'Stray monumental inscriptions to Cheshire people, Caernarvonshire, Llandegai', *C.Sf.* 3rd series **31**, 1937, 13. Cragg family of Mobberley memorial in Caernarvonshire, 19th c.

Egerton
HIGSON, J. 'Egerton inscriptions from a gravestone south side of Aston Chapel, Cheshire', *M.G.H.* N.S., 1, 1874, 18. John Egerton, 1652.
L., V. 'Egerton burials at Little Budworth', *C.Sf.* 3rd series **43**, 1949, 14. 18-19th c.
GREY-EGERTON, PHILIP B. *The Egerton memorial in Chester Cathedral, dedicated July 26, 1921: a page of family history from the record of the war, 1914-1918.* [Tarporley]: privately published, 1921. Includes biographical notes on members of the family who fell; also folded pedigree, 18-20th c.

Fitton
RENAUD, FRANK. 'Memorial brasses of Sir Edward Fitton and Dean Robert Sutton in St. Patricks, Dublin', *L.C.A.S.* 11, 1893, 34-51. 16th c.

Elton
VIATOR. 'A Frodsham of Elton monument', *C.Sf.* 3rd series **14**, 1919, 8. 1752.

Garratt
VIATOR. 'Monumental inscriptions of Chester people in the churchyard of Aston by Frodsham', 21, 1916, 44. Garratt family, 18-19th c.

Glegg
BEAZLEY, F.C. 'Glegg and Cottingham tombstones at Neston', *C.Sf.* 3rd series **6**, 1907, 75. 19th c.

Harding
See Tollemache

Harper
'Henry Harper of Chester and Huntington, gentleman', *C.Sf.* 3rd series **27**, 1934, 866-7. Monumental inscription, 1669, at Chester.

Hassall
S., A.G. 'Hassall monument in St. Johns, Chester', *C.Sf.* 3rd series **37**, 1948, 50-53. 17th c.

Herbert
S., A.G. 'Interesting monument in St. John's church, Chester', *C.Sf.* 3rd series **37**, 1948, 3-4. Edward Herbert, 1688.

Hurlestone
'A Hurlestone monument', *C.Sf.* 3rd series **27**, 1934, 59-60. 17th c., of Chester.

Jenks
B[ENNETT], J.H.E. 'Three vicars of Wybunbury', *C.Sf.* 3rd series 22 1927, 12-13. Inscription to Thomas Jenks, 1700, James Bramfield, 1726 and Thomas Podmore, 1784, with notes on their families.

Johnson
'Two monumental inscriptions in St. Peters church, Chester', *C.Sf.* 3rd series **20**, 1924, 49-50. Johnson family, early 19th c.

Jones

B[ENNETT], J.H.E. 'Family of Jones of Churton', *C.Sf.* 3rd series **20**, 1924, 42-3. Inscriptions, 18th c.

Lingard

CLAYTON, G. 'Some notice of a monumental brass to the memory of Mr. Lingard, in the parish church of Warmingham, Cheshire', *H.S.L.C.* **1**, 1849, 109-11. 1620.

Monksfield

'An old memorial in St. Martin's church, Chester', *C.Sf.* 3rd series **44**, 1950, 27-8. To Richard Monksfield, 1644.

Morgell

'A Morgell of Moston monument in St. Michael's church in Chester', *C.Sf.* 3rd series **27**, 1934, 72-3. 1659.

Oldfield

STEWART-BROWN, R. 'The Oldfield monuments in the church of St. Mary-on-the-Hill, Chester', *C.Sf.* 3rd series **32**, 1938, 3-4. 17-18th c.

Orme

SHELDON, T. STEELE. 'Edward Orme, organist: his mural tablet', *C.Sf.* 3rd series **11**, 1915, 38-9. See also 65 & 70. Of Chester, 1777.

Podmore

See Jenks

Poole

TIMBRELL, W.F.JOAN. 'Arms of Poole in windows at Shotwick and Eastham churches', *C.Sf.* 3rd series **15**, 1920, 62.

Pott

'A stray monumental inscription', *C.Sf.* 3rd series **48**, 1956, 34. Inscription to Edward Pott of Pott, 1650, in Islington church, Middlesex.

Smith

B[ENNETT] J.H.E. 'The Smith monument in Wybunbury church', *C.Sf.* 3rd series **22**, 1927, 11.

Sutton

See Fitton

Tollemache

VIATOR. 'Monumental inscriptions in Tilston Fearnall church', *C.Sf.* 3rd series **16**, 1921, 51-2. Relating to Tollemache, Corbet and Harding families.

Townshend

SMALLWOOD, R.H.G. 'The Townshends of Hem', *C.Sf.* 3rd series **13**, 1918, 42-3. Inscription, 18th c.

Trygarn

S., A.G. 'A stray monumental inscription of a citizen of Chester', *C.Sf.* 3rd series **34**, 1941, 81-2. Trygarn family, 17th c.

Twanbrook

H. 'Twanbrook family', *C.Sf.* 3rd series **13**, 1918, 56. Monumental inscriptions at Daresbury, 18th c.

Vawdrey

OWENS, JOHN. 'Vawdrey inscriptions: Bowdon church, Cheshire', *M.G.H.* N.S., 1 1874, 32-3, 17-18th c.

Welde

'William Welde of Chester', *C.Sf.* **2**, 1883, 378. Monumental inscription, 1656.

Whitby

S., A.G. 'A Whitby mural tablet', *C.Sf.* 3rd series **38**, 1948, 80-81. In Chester, early 17th c.

Whitmore

WILLIAMS, STEPHEN W. 'Effigy in Holy Trinity church, Chester', *J.C.A.H.S.* **6**(1), 1897, 42-8. Of John de Whitmore, 1374.

Wilbraham

S., A.G. 'A stray monumental inscription', *C.Sf.* 3rd series **48**, 1956, 58. To Sir Roger Wilbraham of Woodhey, 1616.

D. *Out of County*

Audley, Staffordshire

H[OUGHTON], B.T. 'Inscription to Cheshire folk at Audley', *C.Sf.* 3rd series **21**, 1926, 86-7. See also 88-9.

Keele, Staffordshire

HOUGHTON, B.T. 'Monumental inscription to Cheshire folk in Staffordshire churches: Keele', *C.Sf.* 3rd series **22**, 1927, 21-2.

Liverpool, Lancashire

H[OUGHTON], B.T. 'Monumental inscriptions to Cheshire folk in the parish church of Our Lady and St. Nicholas, Liverpool', *C.Sf.* 3rd series **23**, 1928, 75-6.

Madeley, Staffordshire

H[OUGHTON], B.T. 'Monumental inscriptions to Cheshire folk in Madeley (Staffordshire) churchyard', *C.Sf.* 3rd series **21**, 1926, 45-6.

7. PROBATE RECORDS AND INQUISITIONS POST MORTEM

A. *General and Indexes*

Probate records - wills, inventories, administration bonds, *etc.,* - constitute another invaluable source of genealogical information. It is usually the case that wills identify all surviving children. There are a number of brief general notes on probate jurisdiction and the uses of wills in Cheshire:

BEAVER, COLIN. 'Some notes on Lancashire and Cheshire wills', *N.C.F.H.* **11**(4), 1984, 37-40. Includes useful hints on searching techniques.

JONES, BRUCE. 'The administration of probate in the Diocese of Chester, 1540-1858', *Society of Local Archivists bulletin* **10**, 1952, 16-21.

STEWART-BROWN, R. 'Probate jurisdiction in Cheshire', *C.Sf.* 3rd series **18**, 1923, 59-60. Brief note.

RICHARDSON, R.C. 'The Diocese of Chester: religion and reading in the late sixteenth and early seventeenth centuries', *Local historian* **11**, 1974, 14-17. Brief note on probate records as a source for information on book ownership.

Most Cheshire wills were proved in the Consistory Court of the Diocese of Chester. Printed indexes to them are available down to 1837. 'Infra' wills, that is, the wills of those who had estates valued at less than £40 are indexed separately in the L.C.R.S. series listed below, since these are kept in separate series. The L.C.R.S. indexes are, however, in the process of being superseded. See:

Wills and other probate records proved in the Chester diocesan consistory court, 1751-1837. 6 vols. Chester: Cheshire Record Office, 1994. A further volume, covering 1701-1750, is in preparation.

EARWAKER, J.P., *An index to the wills and inventories now preserved in the Court of Probate at Chester, from A.D. 1545 to 1620, together with (1) a list of the transcripts of early wills preserved in the Consistory Court, Chester; (2) a list of the wills printed by the Chetham Society; (3) a list of the wills seen and notes by the Revs. J. & G.J. Piccope, and not now to be found at Chester; (4) a list of the wills preserved in Harl. ms. 1991 in the British Museum.* L.C.R.S. **2**. 1879.

IRVINE, WM. FERGUSSON, ed. 'An index to the wills and inventories preserved in the probate register at Chester, commonly called *infra* wills, being those in which the personalty was under £40, between the years 1590 and 1665', in *Miscellanies relating to Lancashire and Cheshire*. **5.** L.C.R.S., **52,** 1906, separately paginated.

EARWAKER, J.P., ed. *An index to the wills and inventories now preserved in the Court of Probate at Chester from A.D. 1621 to 1650, with two appendices: (I) A list of the Lancashire and Cheshire wills proved in the Prerogative Court of Canterbury, 1650-1660; (II) A list of the Lancashire and Cheshire administrations granted in the Prerogative Court of Canterbury, 1650-1660.* L.C.R.S., **4.** 1881.

EARWAKER, J.P., ed. *An index to the wills and inventories now preserved in the Court of Probate at Chester, from A.D.1660-1680, with an appendix containing the list of the 'infra' wills (or those in which the personalty was under £40) between the same years.* L.C.R.S. **15.** 1887. See also supplement for 1670, in L.C.R.S., **63,** 1912, 179-87.

EARWAKER, J.P., ed. *An index to the wills and inventories now preserved in the Court of Probate at Chester, from A.D. 1681 to 1700, with an appendix containing the list of the 'infra' wills (or those in which the personalty was under £40) between the same years.* L.C.R.S.,**18.** 1888. See also supplement for 1693 in L.C.R.S., **63,** 1912, 193-9.

EARWAKER, J.P., ed. *An index to the wills and inventories now preserved in the Court of Probate at Chester, from A.D. 1701 to 1720, with an appendix containing the list of the 'infra' wills . . .* L.C.R.S., **20.** 1889.

EARWAKER, J.P., ed. *An index to the wills and inventories now preserved in the Court of Probate at Chester, from A.D. 1741 to 1760, with an appendix containing the list of the 'infra' wills . . .* L.C.R.S., **25.** 1892.

IRVINE, WM. FERGUSSON. *An index to the wills and inventories now preserved in the Probate Registry at Chester from A.D. 1761 to 1780.* L.C.R.S. **37-8.** 1898-9. The title page of the 2nd volume reads '1741 to 1760' in error.

IRVINE, WM. FERGUSSON, ed. *An index to the wills and inventories now preserved in the Probate Registry at Chester, from A.D. 1781 to 1790, with an appendix containing the list of the 'infra' wills . . .* L.C.R.S. **44.** 1902.

IRVINE, WM. FERGUSSON, ed. *An index to the wills and inventories now preserved in the Probate Registry at Chester, from A.D. 1791 to 1800, with an appendix containing the list of the 'infra' wills . . .* L.C.R.S. **45,** 1902.

STEWART-BROWN, R. *An index to the wills and administrations (including the 'infra' wills) now preserved in the Probate Registry at Chester for the years 1801-1810, both inclusive.* L.C.R.S. **62-3.** 1911-12. Pt.1. A-L. Pt.2. M-Z.

TONGE, WM. ASHETON, ed. *An index to the wills and administrations (including the 'infra' wills) preserved in the Probate Registry at Chester, for the years 1811-1820, both inclusive.* 2 vols. L.C.R.S., **78-9.** 1928.

DICKINSON, ROBERT, ed. *An index to the wills and administrations formerly prserved in the Probate Registry at Chester for the years 1821-1825; both inclusive.* L.C.R.S., **107.** 1961.

DICKINSON, ROBERT, ed. *Index to wills and administrations formerly preserved in the Probate Registry, Chester, 1826-1830.* L.C.R.S. **113.** 1972.

DICKINSON, ROBERT, & DICKINSON, FLORENCE, eds. *Index to wills and administrations formerly preserved in the Probate Registry, Chester, 1831-1833.* L.C.R.S., **118.** 1978. Separately paginated.

DICKINSON, FLORENCE. *Index to wills and administrations formerly preserved in the Probate Registry, Chester, 1834-1837.* L.C.R.S., **120.** 1980.

Other miscellaneous indexes to wills at Chester include:

IRVINE. WM. FERGUSSON. 'An index of the wills, inventories, administration bonds, and depositions in testamentary suits now preserved at the Diocesan Registry, Chester, from 1487 to 1620 inclusive', in *Miscellanies relating to Lancashire and Cheshire*, **3.** L.C.R.S., **33,** 1896, separately paginated.

PRICE, W.H. 'Index to wills, inventories, administration bonds, and depositions, *etc.,* in testamentary suits, preserved in the Diocesan Registry of Chester, 1621-1700', in *Miscellanies relating to Lancashire and Cheshire* **4.** L.C.R.S. **43,** 1902, separately paginated.

PRICE, W.H. 'Calendar of wills, inventories, administration bonds, citations, accounts and depositions in testamentary suits preserved in the Diocesan Registry of Chester, 1701-1800', in *Miscellanies relating to Lancashire and Cheshire* 5. L.C.R.S. **52**, 1906, separately paginated.

Cheshire wills were also proved in the Prerogative Court of Canterbury (P.C.C.) and the Prerogative Court of York (P.C.Y.). For P.C.C. wills, see my *English genealogy: an introductory bibliography,* in addition to *L.C.R.S.* **4**, noted above. For P.C.Y. wills, see: 'Cheshire wills proved at the Prerogative Court of York (P.C.Y.)', *N.C.F.H.* **14**(2), 1987, 38-40. Index, early 19th c., to North Cheshire wills. Wills in the British Library's Harleian manuscripts 1991, 2061 and 2067 are listed in: 'Cheshire and Lancashire, etc., wills', *C.Sf.* 3rd series **26**, 1934, 2-27, *passim.*

See also:
'Cheshire and Lancashire wills', *C.Sf.* 3rd series **27**, 1934, *passim.*

B. *Abstracts: General*

Numerous abstracts of Cheshire wills have been published. Major collections include:

EARWAKER, J.P., ed. *Lancashire and Cheshire wills and inventories at Chester, with an appendix of abstracts of wills now lost or destroyed,* transcribed by the late G.J.Piccope. Cm.S., N.S., **3**, 1884. Abstracts.

IRVINE, WM. FERGUSSON, ed. *A collection of Lancashire and Cheshire wills not now to be found in any probate registry, 1301-1752.* L.C.R.S. **30**. 1896.

PICCOPE, G.J., ed. *Lancashire and Cheshire wills and inventories from the ecclesiastical court, Chester.* Cm.S., O.S., **33, 51 & 54**. 1857-61. v.1. 1525-54. v.2. 1483-1585. v.3. 1596-1639. Transcripts of selected items only.

RYLANDS, J. PAUL, ed. *Lancashire and Cheshire wills and inventories, 1563 to 1807, now preserved at Chester.* Cm.S., N.S., **37**. 1897. Abstracts.

EARWAKER, J.P., ed. *Lancashire and Cheshire wills and inventories, 1572 to 1696, now preserved at Chester, with an appendix of Lancashire and Cheshire wills proved at York or Richmond, 1542 to 1649.* Cm.S., N.S., **28**. 1893.

For abstracts of wills in the Prerogative Court of York, see:

Testamenta Eboracensia, or, wills registered at York illustrative of the history, manners, languages, statistics, etc., of the Province of York, from the year MCCC downwards. Surtees Society **4, 30, 45, 53, 79 & 106**. 1836-1902. Title varies. Pt.1. 1316-1430. Pt.2. 1429-67 (includes index to pt.1) Pt.3. 1395-1491. (also includes marriage licenses). Pt.4. 1420-1509 (also includes marriage licenses *etc.,*). Pt.5. 1509-31. Pt.6. 1516-51.

There are also a mumber of collections of will abstracts *etc.* from particular places:

Burton
CULLEN, MARGARET. 'Burton wills', *Cheshire history* **5**, 1980, 37-45. General discussion of wills from Burton.

Christleton
G.-W., A.A. 'Wills of parishioners of Christleton', *C.Sf.* 3rd series **31**, 1937, *passim.*

Stockport
PHILLIPS, C.B., & SMITH, J.H., eds. *Stockport probate records, 1578-1619.* L.C.R.S. **124**. 1985.

PHILLIPS, C.B., & SMITH, J.H., eds. *Stockport probate records, 1620-1650.* L.C.R.S. **131**. 1992.

C. *Abstracts: Families*

Aldersey
S., A.G. 'Will of John Aldersey of Chester, 1605', *C.Sf.* 3rd series **36**, 1948, 13-14.

Anglezer
B[EAZLEY], F.C. 'Some Cheshire wills', *C.Sf.* 3rd series **21**, 192-6, 86. Will of Matthew Anglezer of Eastham, 1582.

Anglizer
SANDERS, F. 'The will of John Anglizer of Eastham A.D., 1628', *Wirral notes and queries* **2**, 1893, 35-6.

Anyon
'Will of Cicely Anyon of Chester, 1629', *C.Sf.* 3rd series **27**, 1934, 1-2 & 3-4. Includes inventory.

Arderne
'Inventory of James Arderne, Dean of Chester', *C.Sf.* 3rd series **54**, 1959, 37. 1691.

Baguley
'Will of Alexander Baguley, 1541', *C.Sf.* 3rd series **18**, 1923, 111.

Bailey
'An executor's account in 1618', *C.Sf.* 3rd series **56**, 1963, 38-52, *passim*. Accounts of the executors of Humphrey Bailey, 1618.

Ball
B[EAZLEY], F.C. 'Some Cheshire wills', *C.Sf.* 3rd series **21**, 1926, 90. Will of George Ball of Erby, 1592.

B[EAZLEY], F.C. 'Some Cheshire wills', *C.Sf.* 3rd series **21**, 1926, 92. Will of John Ball of Woodchurch, 1604.

B[EAZLEY], F.C. 'Will of William Ball of Chester, glover, 1665', *C.Sf.* 3rd series **22**, 1927, 73-4.

Barnston
I[RVINE], W.F. 'The will of William Barnston of Churton, 1664', *C.Sf.* 3rd series **30**, 1935, 84-8, *passim*.

Barret
'[Will of Margaret Barret of Hanford, 1673]' *F.H.S.C.J.* **6**(1), 1976. Facsimile inside cover. For transcription, see **6**(2), 1977, 12.

Barrington
'The John Barrington will', *Manchester genealogist* **19**(2), 1983, 49. Of Stockport; 1844.

Barrow
B[EAZLEY], F.C. 'Some Cheshire wills', *C.Sf.* 3rd series **21**, 1926, 95. Will of Katherine Barrow of Neston, 108.

Bars
B[ENNET], J.H.E. 'Will of John Bars, 1348', *C.Sf.* 3rd series **21**, 1926, 52. Of Chester.

Batha
B[EAZLEY], F.C. 'Some Cheshire wills', *C.Sf.* 3rd series **22**, 1927, 6. Will of William Batha of Dokinton, Malpas, 1608 (proved 1610).

Bathoe
B[EAZLEY], F.C. 'Some Cheshire wills', *C.Sf.* 3rd series **22**, 1927, 9-10. Will of Thomas Bathoe of Lartonne, 1616.

W., T.L.O. 'Will of Edward Bathoe of Chester', *C.Sf.* 3rd series **9**, 1913, 56. 1628.

Betson
'Will of George Betson of Little Neston, 1745', *C.Sf.* 3rd series **20**, 1924, 72-3.

Beverley
'The will of Sir George Beverley, Knight, of Huntington, near Chester', 1620', *C.Sf.* N.S., **1**, 1895, 151-2.

Bird
'The will of Jane Bird of Chester', *C.Sf.* 3rd series **27**, 1934, 83-4. 1571.

Blackburne
STEWART-BROWN, R. 'Blackburne family', *C.Sf.* 3rd series **8**, 1911, 91. Will of Thomas Blackburne, 1662-3.

Blease
J., E.W. 'An apothecaries inventory in 1631', *C.Sf.* 3rd series **55**, 1960, 5-6. Of Robert Blease.

Bold
B[EAZLEY], F.C. 'Will of Margery Bold of Upton, 1570', *C.Sf.* 3rd series **12**, 1917, 89-90.

Bostock
A., F.S. 'Will of Robert Bostock of Multon, 1537', *C.Sf.* 3rd series **17**, 1922, 88.

HOLLY. 'The will of Robert Bostock of Moulton, in the parish of Davenham, 1537', *C.Sf.* 3rd series **26**, 1934, 35.

A., F.S. 'Will of Henry Bostoke, 1551', *C.Sf.* 3rd series **17**, 1922, 112.

'Will of Henry Bostock of Picton, 1588', *C.Sf.* 3rd series **30**, 1935, 71.

'Will of Ralph Bostock of Huxley, gentleman, 1599', *C.Sf.* 3rd series **30**, 1935, 64.

X. Bostock family of Bruern Stapleford', *C.Sf.* 3rd series **35**, 1948, 32 & 34. Wills, 17th c.

'Will of Anne Bostock of Churton, widow, 1622', *C.Sf.* 3rd series **30**, 1935, 67.

'The Bostocks of Holt', *C.Sf.* 3rd series **23**, 1928, 7-8. Wills, 17th c.

'Bostock family of Farndon', *C.Sf.* 3rd series **26**, 1934, 30-31 & 32-3. Wills of Thomas Bostock, 1636, and Edward Bostock, 1645.

B[EAZLEY], F.C. 'Some Cheshire wills', *C.Sf.* 3rd series **22**, 1927, 50. Will of Cheney Bostock, 1675.

Bosyer
SIMPSON, E. [ed.] 'Transcription of the will', *F.H.S.C.J.* 1(1) 1969, 13-14. Will of Robert Bosyer of Agden, 1680.

Brassye
'A Chester man's will, A.D. 1558', *C.Sf.* N.S., 1, 1880, 289-91. William Brassye, 1558.

Brereton
'Will of Sir Randle Brereton, 1530', *C.Sf.* 3rd series **7**, 1910, 67-9 & 70-71.
A., F.S. 'Will of Randolph Brereton of Chester, 1537', *C.Sf.* 3rd series **17**, 1923, 30.
A., F.S. 'Will of Sir Richard Brereton of Tatton, Kt. 1558', *C.Sf.* 3rd series **17**, 1922, 77-8.
CROSSLEY, FRED. H. 'A disputed Cheshire will of the early 17th century, from the Star Chamber proceedings', *J.C.A.H.S.* N.S., **37**(1), 1948, 141-68. Will of Sir Randal Brereton, 1611.

Brerewood
WOODWARD, D.M. 'Robert Brerewood, an Elizabethan master craftsman', *Cheshire round* **1**(9), 1968, 311-16. Based on his probate inventory, 1601; of Chester.

Bridges
HEWITT, JOHN. 'William Bridges, priest of Macclesfield', *C.Sf.* **3**, 1891, 144-5. Will, 1535.

Brock
See Brooke

Brooke
BEAZLEY, F.C. 'Notes on the Brooke and Brock families of Cheshire', *H.S.L.C.* **74**; N.S., **38**, 158-74. Will abstracts, 16-17th c., also includes folded pedigrees, 16-17th c.
HIDDERLEY, SARAH. 'Hidden names in 17th century wills', *N.C.F.H.* **18**(1), 1991, 8-9. Lists 27 names in the will of John Brooke of Snelson, 1689.

Broughton
'The family of Broughton of Shocklach and Marchwiel in the 16th century. *C.Sf.* 3rd series **27**, 1934, 88-9. See also **28**, 1935, 4. Wills of Ralph Broughton of Shocklach, 1565 and Lancelot Broughton of Eyton, Denbighshire, 1576.

Bruerton
B[EAZLEY] F.C. 'Some Cheshire wills', *C.Sf.* 3rd series **22**, 1927, 13. Will of John Bruerton of Moreton, 1608.

Bryson
A., F.S. 'Will of John Bryson, 1557', *C.Sf.* 3rd series **17**, 1922, 82.

Bulkeley
'Two fifteenth century Bulkeley wills', *C.Sf.* 3rd series **37**, 1948, 54-5 & 62. Wills of Charles Bulkeley of Norbury, 1483, and Thomas Bulkeley of Sandwich, Kent, 1490.

Bunbury
GENEALOGIST. 'The will of Thomas Bunbury of Stanney, esquire, 1600', *C.Sf.* 3rd series **1**, 1896, 44-5.

Burges
B[EAZLEY], F.C. 'Will of Nicholas Burges of Hollingworth, 1635', *C.Sf.* 3rd series **19**, 1924, 48.

Calveley
HISTORICUS. 'The Calveley family of Lea', *C.Sf.* 3rd series **32**, 1938, 43-4. Will of Dorothy Calveley, 1622.
'The will of Dame Mary Caveley of Lea, Co. Chester', *C.Sf.* N.S., **1**, 1895, 117-8. 1701.

Candland
B[EAZLEY], F.C. 'Some Cheshire wills', *C.Sf.* 3rd series **22**, 1927, 15. Will of Randall Candland, of Preen, 1603.

Chalyner
'Will of Richard Chalyn[er] of Chester, 1549', *C.Sf.* 3rd series **19**, 1924, 13.

Chamber
'Will of Jane Chamber of Chester, 1548', *C.Sf.* 3rd series **21**, 1926, 26.
See also Robinson

Chantrell
B[EAZLEY], F.C. 'Some Cheshire wills', *C.Sf.* 3rd series **22**, 1927, 18-19. Will of Marie Chantrell of Knocktorum, 1611 (proved 1613).

Clutton
HALL, JAMES. 'A Cheshire lady's inventory in 1611', *L.G.* 1(7), 1880, 260-66. Probate inventory of Margery Clutton of Nantwich, 1611.

Clyff
A., F.S. 'Will of Robert Clyff, chaplain, 1538', *C.Sf.* 3rd series **18**, 1923, 67-8.

Coker
F., A.J. 'An unrecorded Chester will', *C.Sf.* 3rd series **59**, 1965, 8. Will of William Coker of Chester 1565.

Cooke
'Will of Elizabeth Cooke of Chester, 1681', *C.Sf.* 3rd series **49**, 1956, 21.

Cotgrave
'George Cotgrave's will', *C.Sf.* 3rd series **4**, 1903, 132-3. Early 17th c.

Coventry
B[EAZLEY], F.C. 'Coventry family', *C.Sf.* 3rd series **8**, 1911, 76, 78, 82-3, 84-5, 88, 90, 93, 95 & 96. Mainly wills, 16-17th c.

Crookhall
RYLANDS, J. PAUL. 'The Rev. John Crookhall, rector of Woodchurch, Co. Chester', *Genealogist* N.S., **36**, 1920, 55-6. Will, 1792.
R[YLANDS], J.P. 'The Rev. John Crookhall of Woodchurch', *C.Sf.* 3rd series **16**, 1921, 25-6. See also 36. Will, 1792.

Croughton
'A Chester early will', *C.Sf.* **1**, 1878, 55. Thomas Croughton, 1530.

Crymes
RAYMOND, RAY. 'Will of Richard Crymes', *F.H.S.C.J.* 14(3), 1985, 13. Of London, 1565; probably originally of Witton.

Daryngton
A., F.S. 'Will of Nicholas Daryngton of Wybunbury, 1543', *C.Sf.* 3rd series **18**, 1923, 36.

Davenport
'Will of Ralph Davenport, of Chester, alderman, 1506', *C.Sf.* 3rd series **23**, 1928, 37-8.

'Will of Anne Davenport of Bramhall, widow, 1601, *C.Sf.* 3rd series **20**, 1924, 51.

Davie
B[EAZLEY], F.C. 'Some Cheshire wills', *C.Sf.* 3rd series **22**, 1927, 29. Will of Richard Davie of Mollington Torrett, 1616.

Davies
MAX, L.P. 'The family of Davies of Ashton and Manley', *C.Sf.* 3rd series **27**, 1934, 67. See also 69-71. Will of Robert Davies, 1658.

Davye
A., F.S. 'Will of John Davye, 1558', *C.Sf.* 3rd series **18**, 1923, 42-3. See also **19**, 1924, 12. Of Chester.

Dayne
B[EAZLEY], F.C. 'Some Cheshire wills', *C.Sf.* 3rd series **22**, 1927, 33. Will of William Dayne of Barnston, 1591.

Denson
B[EAZLEY], F.C. 'Denson of Wervin &c', *C.Sf.* 3rd series **14**, 1919, 39, 40, & 47. Probate records and monumental inscriptions, 17-19th c.
B[EAZLEY], F.C. 'Some Cheshire wills', *C.Sf.* 3rd series **22** 1927, 34. Will of John Denson of Whitby, 1617.

Derbishire
B[EAZLEY], F.C. 'Will of Thomas Derbishire of Davenham, clerk, 1745', *C.Sf.* 3rd series **22**, 1927, 75.

Deykyn
B[ENNETT], J.H.E. 'Will of Nicholas Deykyn of Chester, 1518', *C.Sf.* 3rd series **14**, 1919, 8-9.

Dod
HEWITT, JOHN. 'The family of Dod of Tushingham', *C.Sf.* 3rd series **33**, 1939, 62-3. Will of Peter Dod, 1733.

Dodyngton
A., F.S. 'Will of Richard Dodyngton, priest, 1495', *C.Sf.* 3rd series **19**, 1924, 46.

Drihurst
See Pennant

Drinkwater

FLETCHER, W.G.D. 'Peter Drinkwater, alderman of Chester, 1631', *C.Sf.* 3rd series **14**, 1919, 52-3 & 54-5. Will.

Duncalf

'The will of John Duncalf of Mobberley, 1592', *C.Sf.* 3rd series 1898, 19-21.

Egerton

A., F.S. 'Will of William Egerton of Hampton, gentleman, 1508', *C.Sf.* 3rd series **17**, 1922, 21.

Elcock

A., F.S. 'Will of Nicholas Elcock, 1536', *C.Sf.* 3rd series **19**, 1924, 63-4.

Englefield

S., A.G. 'Englefield family', *C.Sf.* 3rd series **29**, 1935, 49-50. Wills of Thomas Englefield of Storeton, 1629 and Thomas Englefield of Woodchurch, 1640.

Fernehed

THOMAS, G.H. 'The will of John Fernehed, A.D. 1565', *Q.J.L.D.* **7**(4), 1984, 6-8.

Fitton

A., M. 'Will of Sir Edward Fitton, 1547-8', *C.Sf.* 3rd series **45**, 1951, 37-8 & 39. Of Gawsworth.

A., F.S. 'Will of Dame Mary Fytton, 1557', *C.Sf.* 3rd series **18**, 1923, 56-7. Of Gawsworth.

'Will of John Fitton of Chester, alderman', *C.Sf.* **2**, 1883, 316. 1605.

'Lancashire and Cheshire wills', *Northern genealogist* **1**, 1895, 228-33. Includes wills of Francis Fitton of Gawsworth, 1608, and Thomas Malbon of Congleton, 1775.

Fletcher

CHORLEY, B.H. 'Inventory of the goods of Richard Fletcher, of Burton, 1617', *Burton and District Local History Society bulletin* **1**, 1977, 5. Includes brief pedigree, 17th c.

'Genealogical abstracts from the wills at the Probate Registry, Chester', *C.Sf.* 3rd series **2**, 1898, 86-7. Wills of William Fletcher of Willaston, 1612, John Meols of Newton, 1628, and John Holland of Little Budworth, 1611.

See also Morris

Forrest

B[EAZLEY], F.C. 'Some Cheshire wills', *C.Sf.* 3rd series **16**, 1921, 27-50, *passim*. Forrest family wills, 17-18th c.

Fouleshurst

A., F.S. 'Will of Sir Robert Fouleshurst, Kt., 1408', *C.Sf.* 3rd series **19**, 1924, 42. Of Barthomley.

Francis

L., P.H. 'Francis family, of Chester and Eastham', *C.Sf.* 3rd series **30**, 1935, 2-31, *passim*. Francis family wills, 16-18th c.

Fyton

A., F.S. 'Will of Richard Fyton, 1438', *C.Sf.* 3rd series **18**, 1923, 24-5.

Gardner

B[EAZLEY], F.C. 'The family of Gardner of Chester', *C.Sf.* 3rd series **14**, 1919, 57, 59 & 60. Wills, 17-18th c.

Gill

'A wealthy miller of Bromborough in 1590', *C.Sf.* 3rd series **53**, 1958, 38-47, *passim*. Will of Thomas Gill, 1590, incluuding extensive list of debtors.

Glasier

M., A. 'William Glasier, mayor of Chester in 1551', *C.Sf.* 3rd series **48**, 1956, 6. Will, 1555.

Gleave

SUMNER, P. 'Names and dwellings in Nantwich, 1765: extracts from the will of Matthew Gleave of Nantwich, gent., 1766, the will being written on November 7, 1765', *F.H.S.C.J.* **7**(1), 1977, 18.

Goodacre

B[ENNETT], J.H.E. 'Will of James Goodacre, 1525', *C.Sf.* 3rd series **20**, 1924, 67. Of Woodchurch.

Goodicar

'The will of John Goodicar, incumbent of Bromborough dated 1623', *Wirral notes and queries* **2**, 1893, 49-50.

Goose

'Will of Thomas Goose of Chester, draper, 1620', *C.Sf.* 3rd series **29**, 1935, 55.

Gravenor

A., F.S. 'Will of Richard Gravenor, of Eton, esq., 1549', *C.Sf.* 3rd series **17**, 1922, 106-7.

A., F.S. 'Will of Sir Thomas Gravener, Kt., 1549, *C.Sf.* 3rd series **17**, 1922, 109-10. Of Eccleston.

Greene

'Thomas Greene of Congleton and Stapley', *C.Sf.* 3rd series **20**, 1924, 36-7 & 38. Will, 1602.

B[EAZLEY], F.C. 'Some Cheshire wills', *C.Sf.* 3rd series **10**, 1914, 8-9. Will of Edward Greene of Poulton Lancelin, 1694.

Griffith

A., F.S. 'Will of Hugh ap Griffith, of Colcot, Co. Ches., 1556/7', *C.Sf.* 3rd series **17**, 1922, 33.

Griffin

B[EAZLEY], F.C. 'Will of John Griffin of Bartherton, esq., 1623', *C.Sf.* 3rd series **20**, 1924, 59-60.

B[EAZLEY], F.C. 'Inventory of Richard Griffin of Bartherton, 1648', *C.Sf.* 3rd series **20**, 1924, 78.

'Will of Ellen Griffin of Mobberley, widow 1669', *C.Sf.* 3rd series **20**, 1924, 76.

B[EAZLEY], F.C. 'Will of Fulk Griffin of Nantwich, 1670', *C.Sf.* 3rd series **20**, 1924, 74.

B[EAZLEY], F.C. 'Will of John Griffin of Nantwich, 1671', *C.Sf.* 3rd series **20**, 1924, 82.

B[EAZLEY], F.C. 'Will of Richard Griffin of Nantwich, esquire, 1690', *C.Sf.* 3rd series **20**, 1924, 61-2.

B[EAZLEY], F.C. 'Admon of Mary Griffin of Badington, widow, 1708', *C.Sf.* 3rd series **20**, 1924, 97.

B[EAZLEY], F.C. 'Will of Thomas Griffin of Nantwich, 1718', *C.Sf.* 3rd series **20**, 1924, 89.

Grosvenor

MAX, L.P. 'Litigation as to the will of Anthony Grosvenor of Doddleston, 1575', *C.Sf.* 3rd series **21**, 1926, 28-30.

MAX, L.P. 'The will of Richard Grosvenor of Eaton, 1620', *C.Sf.* 3rd series **22**, 1927, 83-4.

Hanke

A., F.S. 'Will of Elizabeth Hanke, 1506', *C.Sf.* 3rd series **17**, 1922, 25.

Hanky

A., F.S. 'Will of John Hanky of Churton, 1497', *C.Sf.* 3rd series **17**, 1922, 23.

Harris

'Will of William Harris of Namptwich, yeoman, 1690 *C.Sf.* 3rd series **24**, 1929, 35. i.e. Nantwich.

Harrison

T., J. 'A Cheshire inventory', *C.Sf.* **57**, 1964, 33-4. Probate inventory of George Harrison of Aldford, 1718.

B[ENNETT], J.H.E. 'Will of Samuel Harrison of Tatton, yeoman, 1737',*C.Sf.* 3rd series **20**, 1924, 94-5. Includes notes on family inscriptions.

Hawarden

A., F.S. 'Will of John Hawarden of Chester, 1496', *C.Sf.* 3rd series **17**, 1922, 69-70.

'Will of John Hawarden of Chester 1496 *C.Sf.* 3rd series **23**, 1928, 2-3.

Heath

L., J. 'Some Heath wills, etc', *C.Sf.* 3rd series **19**, 1924, 71. 18th c.

'Will of Richard Heath of Bromhall, farmer, 1774', *C.Sf.* 3rd series **19**, 1924, 73.

Hesketh

'The will of Robert Hesketh of Rycrofte, in Bowdon, Co. Chester, 1516', *C.Sf.* 3rd series **32**, 1938, 48.

Higginbottom

HIGENBOTTOM, FRANK. 'The earliest known Higginbottom will', *N.C.F.H.* 2(2), 1973, 11-13. Will of Alice Higginbottom of Marple, 1594.

Higginson

'Richard Higginson, of Chester, brewer', *C.Sf.* 3rd series **27**, 1934, 23-4. Will, 1701/2; also will of his wife Hannah, proved 1707.

Hockenhull

'Will of Richard Hockenhull of Chester, 1528', *C.Sf.* 3rd series **49**, 1956, 16-19, *passim.*

HOLLY. 'The family of Hockenhull of Prenton', *C.Sf.* 3rd series **20**, 1924, 5-6. Will of John Hockenhull, 1646.
'John Hockenhull of Poole', *C.Sf.* 3rd series **12**, 1917, 82. Will, 1802.

Hocknell
B., J. 'Will of William Hocknell of Prenton, 1563, *C.Sf.* 3rd series **14**, 1919, 32.

Holland
See Fletcher

Holme
See Morris

Holte
B[EAZLEY], F.C. 'Some Cheshire wills', *C.Sf.* 3rd series **16**, 1921, 21. Will of Edward Holte of Sale, 1684.

Hope
A., F.S. 'Will of John Hope of Chester, 1439', *C.Sf.* 3rd series **17**, 1922, 105.

Hough
DODD, J.PHILLIP. 'The inventory of Richard Hough, esq., of Leighton', *Cheshire history* **6**, 1980, 75-82. 1574.

Huntington
'[Will of Margaret Huntington of Lower Bebington, 1681]', *F.H.S.C.J.* **5**(3), 1976 (facsimile inside cover).

Hurdis
R., C.D. 'Peter Hurdis, master of Bowdon school, c. 1616-1672', *C.Sf.* 4th series **2**, 1967, 29-31. Will and probate inventory, 1672.

Huxley
B[ENNETT], J.H.E. 'Will of Rafe Huxley, 1514', *C.Sf.* 3rd series **21**, 1926, 39.

Ince
L., V. 'Will of Nicholas Ince of Chester', *C.Sf.* 3rd series **46**, 1952, 1-2. 1652.
X. 'Will of Thomas Ince of Christleton, 1805', *C.Sf.* 3rd series **35**, 1948, 64-5.

Jannion
B[EAZLEY], F.C. 'Some Cheshire wills', *C.Sf.* 3rd series **16**, 1921, 29. Will of Frances Jannion of Nether Knutsford, 1728.

Johnson
A., F.S. 'Will of Matthew Johnson, *alias* Hewster, 1498-9', *C.Sf.* 3rd series **18**, 1923, 92. Of Chester.
'Will of Thomas Johnson of Great Neston, 1751', *C.Sf.* 3rd series **29**, 1935, 81.

Ketell
B[ENNETT], J.H.E. 'Will of William Ketell, 1361', *C.Sf.* 3rd series **21**, 1926, 44. Of Bunbury.

Larden
'Larden family of Tattenhall and Chester', *C.Sf.* 3rd series **33**, 1939, 27-40, *passim.* Will, 17th c.

Lauton
A., F.S. 'Will of Robert Lauton of Aldford, 1539', *C.Sf.* 3rd series **17**, 1922, 27.

Leche
L., P.H. 'Will of George Leche of the City of Chester, Alderman, 1551', *C.Sf.* 3rd series **20**, 1924, 35-6.
'Will of Henry Leche, of Chester, draper, 1569', *C.Sf.* 3rd series **20**, 1924, 40-41.
L., P.H. 'Will of Rauf Leche of Chester, 1580', *C.Sf.* 3rd series **20**, 1924, 44.
'The will of Dr. Robert Leche, Chancellor of the Diocese of Chester, 1587', *C.Sf.* 3rd series **26**, 1934, 85.

Ledgerd
B., J. 'Will of Alice Ledgerd, 1591', *C.Sf.* 3rd series **12**, 1917, 92.

Legh
THOMAS, G.H. 'Thomas Legh's will', *Q.J.L.D.* **5**(2), 1982 4-5. Of High Leigh, 1589.
B[EAZLEY], F.C. 'Some Cheshire wills', *C.Sf.* 3rd series **1**, 1021, 3-14, passim. Wills of the Legh family of Macclesfield, *etc.* 17th c.
B[EAZLEY], F.C. 'Some Cheshire wills', *C.Sf.* 3rd series **22**, 1927, 49. Will of Peter Legh of Norbury Booths, 1714.
B[EAZLEY], F.C. 'Some Cheshire wills', *C.Sf.* 3rd series **9**, 1913, 70-71. Will of Thomas Legh of High Leigh, 1721.
'Some Cheshire wills', *C.Sf.* 3rd series **9**, 1913, 75-6. Will of Frances Legh of Macclesfield, 1734.

Leghe

HUGHES, E.M. 'The will of Roger Leghe, rector of Lymm, A.D. 1551', *Q.J.L.D.* 3(3), 1980, 9-11.

Leigh

S[TEWART]-B[ROWN], R. 'Will of Richard Leigh of High Leigh', *C.Sf.* 3rd series 12, 1917, 47. 1540-41.

R[YLANDS], J.P. 'Leigh of Thelwall', *C.Sf.* 3rd series 9, 1913, 52-3. Mainly wills, 17th c.

B[EAZLEY], F.C. 'Some Cheshire wills', *C.Sf.* 3rd series 22, 1927, 47-8. Will of Peter Leigh of Lymm Booths, 1690.

Leversage

'The inventory of William Leversage, 1668', *C.Sf.* 3rd series 55, 1960, 9-10.

Levesley

L., P.H. 'Levesley family', *C.Sf.* 3rd series 9, 1913, 23. Will of Robert Lievesley of Chester, 1742.

Leycester

B[EAZLEY], F.C. 'Some Cheshire wills', *C.Sf.* 3rd series 9, 1913, *passim.* Leycester family wills, 16-17th c.

HEWITT, JOHN. 'Will of Rauff Leycester of Toft, Co. Chester', *C.Sf.* 3rd series 13, 1918, 20-21.

Leygh

'Will of Robert Leygh, 1530', *C.Sf.* 3rd series 18, 1923, 5-6. Of Macclesfield.

Ligh

'Will of Dulassa Ligh, widow, 1493', *C.Sf.* 3rd series 19, 1924, 62. See also 20, 1924, 25. Of Stockport.

Liptrott

R., C.D. Will of William Liptrott of Weston near Runcorn, schoolmaster, 1688', *C.Sf.* 4th series 2, 1967, 24-5.

Lloyd

See Morris

Lowndes

B[EAZLEY], F.C. 'Will of John Lowndes of Overton, Co. Chester, gent., 1666', *C.Sf.* 3rd series 20, 1924, 9.

Macclesfield

'The earliest Cheshire will', *C.Sf.* 3rd series 4, 1903, 32-3. Will of Thomas de Macclesfield, 1301.

MAXFIELD, DAVID K. 'The will of John Macclesfield, 1351-1422', *Cheshire history* 22, 1988, 11-14. 1421.

Malbon

See Fitton

Manley

A., F.S. 'Will of Nicholas Manley 1520-1', *C.Sf.* 3rd series 17, 1922, 94-5. Of Pulton.

Marbury

'Will of John Marbury, rector of Davenham, County Chester, 1724', *C.Sf.* 3rd series 8, 1911, 8-9.

Massey

A., F.S. 'Will of Ralph Massie, esquire, 1495', *C.Sf.* 3rd series 17, 1922, 55.

A., F.S. 'Will of John Mascy of Coddington, 1499', *C.Sf.* 3rd series 17, 1922, 39.

A., M. 'The will of Richard Mascy of Grafton, 1505', *C.Sf.* 3rd series 50, 1958, 4.

A., F.S. 'Will of Edmund Mascy, priest, 1517', *C.Sf.* 17, 1922, 59.

B[EAZLEY], F.C. 'Some Cheshire wills', *C.Sf.* 3rd series 23, 1928, 41-64, *passim.* Wills of Massey or Mascie family, 17th c.

'Abstracts of wills at the Probate Registry, Chester', *C.Sf.* 3rd series 1, 1896, 56. Wills of Richard Massey of Coggeshall, 1663, John Massey of Great Saughall, 1677, and Thomas Meoles of Wallasey, 1663.

Mather

B[ENNETT], J.H.E. 'The Mather family of Chester', *C.Sf.* 3rd series 20, 1924, 10-11 & 12-13. Includes will of John Mather, 1700, with 18th c. pedigree.

Maynwaring

A., F.S. 'Will of Sir John Maynwaring of Over Peover, Kt., 1516', *C.Sf.* 3rd series 17, 1922, 73.

A., F.S. 'Will of Nicholas Maynwaring, clerk 1537', *C.Sf.* 3rd series 17, 1922, 75-6.

Meoles

See Massey

Meols
See Fletcher

Merbury
A., F.S. 'Will of James Merbury, 1457', *C.Sf.* 3rd
series **19**, 1924, 39.

Middleton
A., F.S. 'Will of Thomas Myddelton, 1535/6',
C.Sf. 3rd series **18**, 1923, 87. Of Chester.
A., F.S. 'Will of David Middelton, 1548', *C.Sf.*
3rd series **18**, 1923, 88-9. Of Chester.
B[EAZLEY], F.C. 'Some Cheshire wills', *C.Sf.*
3rd series **21**, 1926, 79. Will of Peter
Middleton of Whitby, in Eastham parish,
1607-8.

Milner
B[EAZLEY], F.C. 'Some Cheshire wills', *C.Sf.* 3rd
series **21**, 1926, 84. Will of Richard Milner of
Little Neston, 1620.

Milton
MARSH, JOHN FITCHET. ed. 'Papers connected
with the affairs of Milton and his family', in
Chetham miscellanies 1. Cm.S., O.S. **24**. 1851.
Separately paginated. Probate records, with
various deeds, 17th c.
'Mrs. Elizabeth Milton', *South Cheshire
Family History Society quarterly journal* **1**,
1990, 7-9. Of Nantwich; will 1727.

Minshull
L., P.H. 'Minshull wills', *C.Sf.* 3rd series **16-18**,
1921-3, *passim.* 16-17th c.
L., P.H. 'Mynshull of Chester', *C.Sf.* 3rd series
12, 1917, 22. Will of Ann Mynshull,
1685/6.
'Will of John Minshull of Chester, 1727', *C.Sf.*
3rd series **25**, 1931, 80-81.
S., R.H.G. 'John Minshull of Coddington, 1754',
C.Sf. 3rd series **12**, 1917, 42. Will.

Mollineux
'The will of Thomas Mollineux, rector of
Wallasey, died A.D. 1549', *W.N.Q.* **2**, 1893,
11-12.

Morgell
B[EAZLEY], F.C. 'Will of Edward Morgell of
Chester, gent., 1661/2', *C.Sf.* 3rd series **19**,
1924, 94.

Morris
HEWITT, JOHN. 'Seals used upon wills, proved
at Chester', *C.Sf.* 3rd series **28**, 1935, 66.
Brief extract from the wills of Anne Morris,
1708, William Harvey, 1684, John Fletcher,
1665, John Lloyd, 1674-5, Robert Harvey,
1669, Randle Holme, 1704, and William
Woods, 1699. (all of Chester, except Woods
of Handbridge)

Morton
'Will of William Morton of Moreton, esquire,
1525', *C.Sf.* 3rd series **18**, 1923, 17-18.

Moss
See Strettill

Newhall
A., F.S. 'Will of Thomas Newhall, 1499', *C.Sf.*
3rd series **18**, 1923, 26.

Norris
B[ENNETT], J.H.E. 'Will of John Norris,
gentleman, 1499', *C.Sf.* 3rd series **22**, 1927,
62.

Orme
ORME, JOHN. 'Hidden names in 17th century
wills', *N.C.F.H.* **20**(1), 1992, 25-8. Indexes
names appearing in pre-1700 wills of the
Orme family of Prestbury.

Orrell
F., H.B. 'Robert Orrell of Ashley, gent', *C.Sf.*
3rd series **18**, 1923, 10. Will, 1810.

Oulegreve
A., F.S. 'Will of Thomas Oulegreve, 1472', *C.Sf.*
3rd series **18**, 1923, 15.

Parr
'Abstracts of wills at the Probate Registry,
Chester', *C.Sf.* 3rd series **2**, 1896, 144-5. Wills
of John Parr of Trafford, 1585, and Richard
Richardson of Little Sutton, 1611.

Parson
'Parson family of Huxley and Beeston', *C.Sf.*
3rd series **13**, 1918, 93-4. Will of Thomas
Parson, 1716.

Partington
B[EAZLEY], F.C. 'Will of Katherine Partington of Cotton, widow, 1593', *C.Sf.* 3rd series **12**, 1917, 88.

Paulden
B[EAZLEY], F.C. 'Some Cheshire wills', *C.Sf.* 3rd series **17**, 1922, 1-19, *passim;* **19**, 1924, *passim.* Paulden family wills, 17th c.

Penkett
'The will of a dictatorial parent in Raby, 1616', *C.Sf.* 3rd series **54**, 1959, 7-8. Will of Thomas Penkett.

Pennant
C., E.R. 'Will of Grace Pennant *alias* Drihurst, of Christleton, widow, 1599', *C.Sf.* 3rd series **26**, 1934, 73.

Powell
'Will of Edward Powell, 1666', *C.Sf.* 4th series **3**, 1968, 9. Of Macclesfield.

Ratcliffe
'Will of Nicholas Ratcliffe of Chester, notary public, 1644', *C.Sf.* 3rd series **60**, 1966, 51.

Rayneforde
A., F.S. 'Will of Henry Rayneforde, chaplain, 1506', *C.Sf.* 3rd series **18**, 1923, 93-4.

Raynshay
A., F.S. 'Will of Richard Raynshay, 1510', *C.Sf.* 3rd series **19**, 1924, 59. Of Ashton.

Redich
A., F.S. 'Will of Robert Redich of Grappenhall, 1508', *C.Sf.* 3rd series **18**, 1923, 61.

Richardson
See Parr

Robinson
B[ENNETT], J.H.E. 'Will of Hugh Robinson *alias* Chamber of Chester, 1535', *C.Sf.* 3rd series **21**, 1926, 9.

Rogers
A., F.S. 'Will of Ralph Rogers 1539/40', *C.Sf.* 3rd series **18**, 1923, 99-100. Of Chester.

Rogerson
'Will of William Rogerson of Chester, 1519', *C.Sf.* 3rd series **13**, 1918, 90-91.

Roncorne
A., F.S. 'Will of Thomas Roncorne, clerk, rector of Bebington, 1557', *C.Sf.* 3rd series **18**, 1923, 55-66.

Runcorn
'Will of Thomas Runcorn 1511', *C.Sf.* 3rd series **15**, 1920, 23.
'The Rev. Richard Runcorn, curate of Upton in Overchurch, 1634-1636', *C.Sf.* 3rd series **29**, 1935, 82-83. Will, 1652.

Ryle
A., F.S. 'Will of Roger Ryle, 1511', *C.Sf.* 3rd series **17**, 1922, 64.
A., F.S. 'Will of Henry Ryle, 1536', *C.Sf.* 3rd series **18**, 1923, 34-5. Of Winslow.

Sandford
'The will of Robert Sandford of Chester, clerk, 1622, *C.Sf.* N.S., **1**, 1895, 140.

Sefton
'The Sefton family of Great Mollington', *C.Sf.* 3rd series **54**, 1959, 12. Will of Myles Sefton, 1578.

Sharpe
'The Rev. Peter Sharpe, rector of Doddleston, 1596-1616', *C.Sf.* series **27**, 1934, 82. Will of Peter Sharpe, 1616, and his widow Julian, 1616.

Sherlock
'The will of Richard Sherlock, D.D.', *Wirral notes and queries* **1**, 1892, 71 & 72, 1689.

Shukburgh
'Will of Marmaduke Shukburgh of Chester, 1680, *C.Sf.* 3rd series **28**, 1935, 11-12.

Simcock
'The will of the Rev. Randle Simcock, curate of Christleton, 1542', *C.Sf.* 3rd series **1**, 1896, 87-8.

Smith
SMITH, RICHARD B.L. 'Wills of Smith families', *N.C.F.H.* **13**(2), 1986, 61-3; 13(3), 1986, 71-2. Of Mottram and Stockport.

s., A.G. 'Will of Elizabeth Smith of Chester, 1682', *C.Sf.* 3rd series **34**, 1941, 105-6.

Snell
'Snell and Vyner families', *C.Sf.* 3rd series **1**, 1896, 111-13. Wills, 17th c.

Spencer
B[ENNETT], J.H.E. 'Will of Nicholas Spencer of Northwich, 1510', *C.Sf.* 3rd series **15**, 1920, 11.

Spurstowe
A., F.S. 'Will of John Spurstowe of Spurstowe, 1539/40', *C.Sf.* 3rd series **17**, 1922, 44-5.
A., F.S. 'Will of Randle Spurstowe of Spurstow, 1527', *C.Sf.* 3rd series **17**, 1922, 42.

Standish
B[ENNETT], J.H.E. 'Alexander Standish, clerk', *C.Sf.* 3rd series **13**, 1918, 81-2. Will, 1538.

Stanley
BURTT, JOSEPH. 'Original documents: will of Sir John Stanley of Honford, Cheshire, dated 20 June, A.D. 1527', *Archaeological journal* **25**, 1868, 72-84.
HOLLY. 'Dame Joan Stanley of Hooton', *C.Sf.* 3rd series **27**, 1934, 26-7. Will, 1614.
W., T.L.O. 'Will of William Stanley of Hooton, 1788', *C.Sf.* 3rd Series **8**, 1911, 10.

Starky
A., F.S. 'Will of Humfry Starky, Kt., 1486', *C.Sf.* 3rd series **17**, 1922, 49-50.
A., F.S. 'Will of Hugh Starky of Oulton, esquire, 1555', *C.Sf.* 3rd series **17**, 1922, 95-6.

Stiles
B[ENNETT], J.H.E. 'Will of William Stiles of Chester, 1585', *C.Sf.* 3rd series **14**, 1919, 13-14 & 17.

Strettill
FORRER, H.B. 'Strettill and Moss families', *C.Sf.* 3rd series **27**, 1934, 81-9, *passim.* Wills, 17th c., of Mobberley.
F[ORRER], H.B. 'Will of Hugh Strettill of Mobberley, 1682', *C.Sf.* 3rd series **20**, 1924, 90-91. Includes family inscriptions.

Sutton
A., F.S. 'Will of Sir Richard Sutton, Kt., 1524', *C.Sf.* 3rd series **17**, 1922, 89-90.

Swettenham
EARWAKER, J.P. 'Lawrence Swettenham of Bradwall, Co. Chester, 1632', *C.Sf.* **3**, 1891, 73-4. Wills.
'Two Swettenham wills', *C.Sf.* 3rd series **26**, 1934, 27. Wills of Thomas Swetnam of Swetnam, 1657, and Thomas Swettenham of Bertles, 1657.

Thomson
B[EAZLEY], F.C. 'Admon. of Rev. Wm. Thomson of Norbury, 1760', *C.Sf.* 3rd series **20**, 1924, 105.

Tilson
'Will of Thomas Tilson of Rushton, 1426', *C.Sf.* 3rd series **17**, 1922, 53.

Toft
'Will of John de Toft, chaplain, 1421', *C.Sf.* 3rd series **18**, 1923, 12-13.

Trafford
B[EAZLEY], F.C. 'Will of William Trafford of Stoak, husbandman, 1578', *C.Sf.* 3rd series **20**, 1924, 33.
B[EAZLEY], F.C. 'Will of Robert Trafford of Bridge Trafford, 1610', *C.Sf.* 3rd series **20**, 1924, 51.
B[EAZLEY], F.C. 'Will of Richard Trafford of Chester, tallow chandler, 1663', *C.Sf.* 3rd series **20**, 1924, 53-4.

Verdon
A., F.S. 'Will of John Verdon, page of the buttery, 1522', *C.Sf.* 3rd series **17**, 1922, 65-6.

Vyner
See Snell

Walker
A., F.S. 'Will of Richard Walker of Congleton, 1508', *C.Sf.* 3rd series **18**, 1923, 64-5.

Walsham
A., F.S. 'Will of William Walsham, 1389', *C.Sf.* 3rd series **18**, 1923, 103. Of Bunbury.

Warde
A., F.S. 'Will of William Warde of Rydmarley, 1503', *C.Sf.* 3rd series **18**, 1923, 22.

Warrington
'Some seventeenth century Cheshire wills', *L.C.A.S.* **46**, 1929, 107-11. Warrington family wills, mid-17th c.

Werham
A., F.S. 'Will of Lawrence Werham (Weverham), 1488', *C.Sf.* 3rd series **18**, 1923, 30-31.

Weverham
See Werham

Whitfield
WHITFIELD, DEREK. 'Some of the names mentioned in the will of Richard Whitfield of Tattenhall, County Chester, yeoman, 1711', *F.H.S.C.J.* **14**(2), 1984, 10.

Whitley
B[EAZLEY], F.C. Whitley of Alvanley pedigree', *C.Sf.* 3rd series **25**, 1931, 15-40, *passim.* Wills, 17-18th c.

Whittle
W., H. 'Richard Whittell of Ashton, Co. Ches., husbandman', *C.Sf.* 3rd series **25**, 1932, 30. Will, 1615; includes list of debtors.
'Whittle family of Oscroft', *C.Sf.* 3rd series **27**, 1934, 21-2. Wills *etc.,* 17-18th c.
W., H.M. 'Ralph Whitle of Childer Thornton', *C.Sf.* 3rd series **27**, 1934, 73 & 76. Will, 1599, with pedigree of 17th c. descendants.
B[EAZLEY], F.C. 'Will of Thomas Whittle of Whitby', *C.Sf.* 3rd series **27**, 1934, 47. 1630.
'Robert Whittle of Bromborough, husbandman', *C.Sf.* 3rd series **25**, 1931, 62-3. Notes on will, 1638.

Wiggan
'The will of a monk of Hilbree Island', *C.Sf.* 3rd series **4**, 1903, 2-3. Will of Robert Wiggan, 1550.
A., F.S. 'Will of Robert Wiggan, clerk, 1550', *C.Sf.* 3rd series **18**, 1923, 75.
'The will of an early rector of West Kirby', *C.Sf.* 3rd series **4**, 1903, 12-13. See also **27**, 1934, 13. Will of William Wiggan, 1526.

Wilbraham
A., F.S. 'Will of William Wilbraham of Woodhey, 1536', *C.Sf.* 3rd series **17**, 1922, 68-9.

Williams
B[ENNETT], J.H.E. 'Kendrick Williams of Chester, ironmonger', *C.Sf.* 3rd series **18**, 1923, 47. Will, 1664.

Wittour
A., F.S. 'Will of William Wittour, clerk, of Tarporley, 1543', *C.Sf.* 3rd series **17**, 1922, 86.

Wood
A., F.S. 'Will of George Wood of Balterley, esq., 1558', *C.Sf.* 3rd series **19**, 1924, 73-4.

Woods
See Morris

Worthington
ROGERS, COLIN. 'Roger Worthington of Etchells, an early Cheshire schoolmaster, *C.Sf.* 4th series **2**, 1967, 6. Probate inventory, 1614.

Wright
F[ORRER], H.B. 'Will of Thomas Wright the elder of Over Peover, yeoman, 1710', *C.Sf.* 3rd series **20**, 1924, 84-5.
F[ORRER], H.B. 'Will of Peter Wright of Over Peover, gent.', *C.Sf.* 3rd series **20**, 1924, 86. 1726/7 (proved 1737). Includes family inscriptions.

Wyche
B[EAZLEY], F.C. 'The Wyche family of Alderley', *C.Sf.* 3rd series **24**, 1929, 72-88, *passim;* **25**, 1931, 1-12, *passim,* & 90-91. Wills, 17-19th c.

Wynne
IRVINE, WM. FERGUSSON. 'An early Bidston will', *C.Sf.* 3rd series **5**, 1906, 6. Will of David Wynne, 1571.
B[EAZLEY], F.C. 'The Wynne family', *C.Sf.* 3rd series **11**, 1915, 31-54, *passim.* Wills, 16-17th c.

Younge
F., A.J. 'An unrecorded Chester will', *C.Sf.* **59**, 1965, 10. Will of Richard Younge of Chester, 1556.

D. *Inquisitions Post Mortem*

Inquisitions post mortem are invaluable sources of information from the medieval period until 1646, when wills are frequently not available. They record the possessions of those who held lands as 'tenants in chief' of the Crown, and are particularly useful in tracing manorial descents. Inquisitions in the Palatinate of Chester are indexed in:

RHODES, E.H. 'Welsh records: index to inquisitions &c., counties of Cheshire and Flint', *Twenty-fifth annual report of the Deputy Keeper of the Public Records* 1864, 32-60.

'Inquisitions post mortem: Palatinate of Chester Henry VIII to Charles II', *Lists and indexes* **33**, 1909, 381-95.

A mumber of works provide abstracts:

BOOTH, P.H.W. 'A Calendar of the Cheshire *inquisitions post mortem* of the thirteenth and fourteenth centuries', *Cheshire history* **19**, 1987, 7-9.

BOOTH, P.H.W. 'The Palatinate of Chester *inquisitions post mortem'*, *Cheshire history* **18**, 1986, 6-9; **27**, 1991, 3-5; **29**, 1992, 3-5. Calendar, 14th c. To be continued.

STEWART-BROWN, R., ed. *Cheshire inquisitions post mortem, Stuart period, 1603-1660.* 3 vols. L.C.R.S., **84, 86** & **91**. 1934-8. Extensive.

A number of inquisitions have been published individually:

Bebington
'The *inquisition post mortem* of Henry Bebington of Bebington, dated 1403', *C.Sf.* 3rd series **2**, 1898, 87.

De La Pole
'Documents relating to Nether Peover', *C.Sf.* 3rd series **3**, 1901, 5-6. *Inquisition post mortem* for John De Le Pole, 1396.

Glegg
IRVINE, WM. FERGUSSON. 'The *inquisition post mortem* of Gilbert Glegg of Gayton dated 1428', *C.Sf.* 3rd series **2**, 1898, 95-6.

Meols
HOLLY. *'Inquisitions post mortem* relating to the family of Meols of Great Meols and Wallasey', *C.Sf.* 3rd series **15**, 1920, 12-13, 14-15 & 18. 16th c.

Whitmore
I[RVINE], W.F. *'Inquisition post mortem* of John Whitmore of Chester and Thurstaston', *C.Sf.* 3rd series **1**, 1896, 27. 1438.

8. OFFICIAL LISTS OF NAMES

A sure sign of the development of government bureaucracy are lists of names. They are needed for a multitude of purposes: defence, taxation, voting, *etc., etc.* Where such lists survive, they are invaluable to genealogists, since they enable the identification of ancestors in time and place. The earliest surviving list is the well-known Domesday book. It is unlikely that you will be able to trace your ancestors that far back - but you never know! For Cheshire, two editions of this record are readily available:

MORGAN, PHILIP, ed. *Domesday book, 2: Cheshire.* Chichester: Phillimore, 1978.

TAIT, JAMES, ed. *The Domesday survey of Cheshire.* Cm.S., N.S., 75. 1916.

A. *Taxation Lists*

From the medieval period until the seventeenth century, the subsidy provided one of the principal sources of government revenue: the tax was paid by heads of households. Unfortunately, there is no edition of the subsidy returns covering the whole county; however, a number of transcripts are available for particular places. These are mainly quite brief.

Broxton Hundred
'The collection of subsidy money in 1642', *C.Sf.* 3rd series 54, 1959, 42-3. Brief extracts relating to Broxton Hundred.

Bucklow Hundred
S[TEWART]-B[ROWN]. R. 'Subsidy rolls of Bucklow Hundred, 1593 and 1663', *C.Sf.* 3rd series 28, 1935, *passim.*

Macclesfield Hundred
DRIVER, JOHN T. 'A subsidy roll for the Hundred of Macclesfield', *L.C.A.S.* 62, 1950-51, 54-67. Transcript.

Wirral Hundred
IRVINE, WM. FERGUSSON, ed. 'Wirral subsidy roll for 1545', *Wirral notes and queries* 1-2, 1892-3, *passim.*

IRVINE, W. FERGUSSON, ed. 'The subsidy roll for 1625', *Wirral notes and queries* 1, 1892, 47, 49, 52, & 53. For the Hundred of Wirral.

The subsidy was replaced by the hearth tax following the restoration of Charles II. Again there is no published edition covering the whole county, but transcripts for a number of particular places are available. Those for Chester, and more especially for the Hundred of Northwich, are quite extensive.

Aston by Budworth
ANTROBUS, R.L. 'Inhabitants of the township of Aston-by-Budworth', *C.Sf.* 3rd series 16, 1921, 57-64, *passim.* Hearth tax returns, 1662-3, 1664 and 1673-4.

Broxton Hundred
BEAZLEY, F.C. 'Hearth tax returns for the Hundred of Broxton, 1663', *C.Sf.* 3rd series 14, 1919, *passim.*

Chester
GAMON, GILBERT P. 'The Chester hearth tax 1663-4', *C.Sf.* 3rd series 4, 1903, 57-8 & 59-61. Partial transcript listing those with 4 or more hearths.

BEAZLEY, F.C, ed. 'Hearth tax returns for the city of Chester preserved in the Public Record OFfice, London', in *Miscellanies relating to Lancashire and Cheshire 5.* L.C.R.S. 52. 1906. Separately paginated.

MORRISON, E.J.D. 'The hearth tax in Chester', *J.C.A.H.S.* N.S., 36(1), 1946, 31-43. General discussion based on Beazley's transcript.

Eddisbury Hundred
B[EAZLEY], F.C. 'Hearth taxes, Eddisbury Hundred', *C.Sf.* 3rd series 7, 1910, *passim.* Transcript, 1663.

BEAZLEY, F.C. 'Hearth taxes, Eddisbury Hundred, 1664', *C.Sf.* 3rd series 11-13, 1915-18, *passim.* Returns for those parishes not covered in 1663.

High Legh
JACKSON, MICHAEL. 'The levy of a hearth tax', *Q.J.L.D.* 2(4), 1979, 11-15. Transcript for High Legh, Thelwall and Warburton, 1673 and 1674.

Lymm
JACKSON, MICHAEL N. 'Hearth tax assessment of Lymm', *N.C.F.H.* 5(2), 1978, 46-9. Transcript, 1673-4.

Lymm *continued*
JACKSON, MICHAEL. 'Hearth Tax assessments of Lymm, 1673 and 1674', *Q.J.L.D.* 2(2), 1979, 166-21.

Northwich Hundred
LAWTON, G.O, ed. *Northwich Hundred: poll tax 1660 and hearth tax 1664.* L.C.R.S. 119, 1979.

Wirral Hundred
'Hearth Taxes, Hundred of Wirral, 1663', *C.Sf.* 3rd series 8-9, 1911-13, *passim.*

The land tax replaced the hearth tax at the end of the seventeenth century. It has not received as much attention from editors as the subsidy or the hearth tax, and only a few returns are in print.

Ashton upon Mersey
'[Land tax assessment, Higher Ashton, 1719]' *F.H.S.C.J.* 6(2), 1977. Facsimile inside cover.

Bromborough
'The Bromborough land taxes', *Lancashire and Cheshire historian* 1, 1965, 19-20, 35-6, 61-2, 83-4, 109-10, 133-4, 159-60, 181-2, 203-4, & 229-30. For 1778-1831.

Dodleston
'Land Tax about 1780', *C.Sf.* 3rd series 47, 1953. 45-7, *passim.* Lists taxpayers for Dodleston and locality.

Lymm
JACKSON, MICHAEL. 'The Lymm land tax assessments', *J.L.D.L.H.S.* 1(2), 1985, 1-11. Transcripts for 1735, 1741 and 1751.
JACKSON, MICHAEL N. 'The Lymm land tax assessments', *N.C.F.H.* 13(3), 1986, 82-5. Includes 1799 assessment.

West Kirby
'Assessment of land tax for the township of West Kirby', *F.H.S.C.J.* 5(2), 1976. Facsimile inside cover.

Wirral Hundred
'Land tax assessments, 1785: Wirral Hundred', *F.H.S.C.J.* 5(3), 1976, 9-10.

A few other minor levies have also left records which have been printed:

GRAY, HENRY. 'The list of those who contributed to the defence of this country at the time of the Spanish Armada in 1588: Cheshire', *C.N.Q.* 6, 1886, 201.
'A kalender conteyning the names of all such gent. and others as upon Her Maty's pryvye seales have paid there money to the hondes of Sir Hugh Cholmondley, Knyghte, collectr of Her Hyghnes loane within the countie of Chester together with the severall somes and daies of receipt, A.D. 1597', in *Chetham miscellanies* 4. Cm.S., O.S., 83. 1872. Separately paginated.
OGDEN, E., & TUPLING, G.H. 'Assessed taxation in Ashton-upon-Mersey in 1821', *L.C.A.S.* 61, 1949, 137-60. Includes list of 75 taxpayers. The only published transcript of the assessed taxes on houses, windows, servants, carriages, horses, dogs, and composition duties that I have seen.

B. *Muster Rolls and Analogous Documents.*
Every adult male in pre-industrial England was required to fight in defence of the realm, and musters were regularly held - although on occasion a financial levy was substituted. A number of the resultant documents have been published:
IRVINE, WM. FERGUSSON IRVINE, ed. 'A list of the freeholders in Cheshire in the year 1578', in *Miscellanies relating to Lancashire and Cheshire* 4. L.C.R.S. 43. 1902. Separately paginated. Assessment of horses and armour.
MAYER, JOSEPH. 'On the arming of levies in the Hundred of Wirral, in the County of Chester, and the introduction of small fire arms as weapons of war in place of bows and arrows', *H.S.L.C.* 11, 1859, 83-96. Includes muster roll, 1587, naming those mustered.
'The light horse of Cheshire', *C.S.* 3. 1883, 106-7. Muster roll, 1660.
'Cheshire Lieutenancy papers, no. VIII: the Light Horse', *C.Sf.* 1, 1879, 231-3. Muster roll, 1666.

C. *Oaths of Allegiance.*
At times of unrest, when governments have been concerned about the loyalties of their subjects, the latter have been required to take oaths of allegiance, sometimes by signing their names. A few Cheshire returns from such oaths have been printed, and are listed here chronologically.

JACKSON, MICHAEL. 'A brief account of the Lymm Protestation of 1641', *Q.J.L.D.* 4(2), 1982, 8-11. Reprinted in *N.C.F.H.* 14(1), 1987, 7-11. Lists 145 names.

IRVINE, WM. FERGUSSON. 'The Solemn League and Covenant in Wirral', *Wirral notes and queries* 1, 1892, 58. Lists signatories, 1646, at Woodchurch.

'The Association of 1696', *C.Sf.* 31-3, 1937-9, *passim.*

MERRELL, BERTRAM. *Cheshire residents in 1723 according to the oaths of allegiance.* 2 fiche. [Salt Lake City, 1981.]

D. *The Franchise.*

Eighteenth and nineteenth-century poll books list those claiming the right to vote, and show how their votes were excercised. Full details of these cannot be given here; reference should be made to the works listed in my *English Genealogy: an introductory bibliography.* A number of extracts from poll book and electoral registers have been published in historial journals; see:

'The Parliamentary election, 1727', *C.Sf.* 3rd series 3, 1901, *passim.* Lists Wirral electors.

'The Parliamentary election 1727', *C.Sf.* 3rd series 2, 1898, 45-6 & 52-3. Lists voters in the townships surrounding Chester.

JACKSON, MICHAEL. 'The Mid-Cheshire by-election of 1873', *Q.J.L.D.* 2(1), 1978, 1-14. Lists voters.

JACKSON, MICHAEL,N. 'The Mid-Cheshire by-election of 1873', *N.C.F.H.* 4(3), 1977, 75-8. Lists voters surnames for Lymm.

For the Macclesfield pollbook of 1804, see under Macclesfield in section 9A.

E. *The Census*

By far the most useful official lists of names are the census enumerators' schedules of the nineteenth century. Works on these are listed here chronologically and by place. For a general introduction see:

WAY, DEREK, H. *Cheshire census of 1841, 1851, 1861, 1871 and 1881: a general introduction to the censuses: where to find your Cheshire village on census.* Macclesfield: D.H. Way, 1984.

See also:

Street indexes, surname indexes & transcripts for 1841-1891 census returns held at Cheshire Record Office, August 1994. Chester: Chester Record Office, 1994.

1801

Pownall Fee

'Census of Pownall Fee for year 1801', *C.N.Q.* 9, 1889, 117-9. 1801 census return for Styal and Morley.

1821

Newton

'Inhabitants of Newton by Chester in 1821', *C.Sf.* 3rd series 13, 1918, 63-4. List, probably from the 1821 census.

Rostherne

'Index of surnames recorded in the 1821, Rostherne parish', *F.H.S.C.J.* 1(2), 1970, 14; 1(3), 1970, 13-14; 1(4), 1970, 14.

1841

Barnton

BUCHAN, G.H. '1841 census for Barnton, Cheshire: index of surnames appearing', *F.H.S.C.J.* 3(4) 1972, 14.

Bramhall Hall

'Census returns for Bramhall Hall', *N.C.F.H.* 6(3), 1979, 73-4. For 1841, 1851, 1861 and 1871.

Burton

'Surnames appearing in the 1841 census of Burton, Cheshire', *F.H.S.C.J.* 2(4), 1971, 3; 3(2), 1972, 12.

Hoylake

'1841 census, Hoylake (Hoose Ward)', *F.H.S.C.J.* 8(2), 1979, 11-12. Lists people born out of Cheshire.

Knutsford

GAUTREY, ARTHUR J. 'Knutsford's prison population, 1841', *N.C.F.H.* 4(3), 1977, 66-9. Census listing of 316 prisoners in the House of Correction.

Lymm

JACKSON, MICHAEL. 'Property ownership in Lymm, 1841-1871', *Q.J.L.D.* 3(1), 1979, 11-16. Census schedules.

Puddington

'Surnames appearing in the 1841 census of Puddington, Cheshire', *F.H.S.C.J.* 2(4), 1971, 3; 3(2), 1972, 12.

South Halton

CAPENER, J.S.A., & KNEEBONE, H.R. *A transcript of the 1841 census returns for the townships of Acton Grange, Aston by Sutton, Aston Grange, Clifton, Daresbury, Norton, Preston, Stockham, Sutton and Weston.* Halton historical publications 5. Halton: Halton Borough Council, 1987. Cover: South Halton.

1851

Surname index: 1851 census of Cheshire. 12 vols. F.H.S.C. & N.C.H.F.S., 1985-91. v.1-2. Stockport Registration District. v.3-4. Macclesfield R.D. v.5. Altrincham R.D. v.6. Runcorn R.D. (published by Liverpool & S.W. Lancashire F.H.S.) v.7. Northwich R.D. v.8. Congleton R.D. v.9. Nantwich R.D. v.10. Chester (Great Broughton) R.D. v.11. Wirral R.D. v.12. Birkenhead & Tranmere R.D.

Index of surnames, 1851 census: P.R.O.Bundle no.HO 107/2203. Warrington: Liverpool & District Family History Society, Warrington Group, 1985. This covers the Warrington Rural District, which included the Cheshire townships of Grappenhall, Latchford and Thelwall.

PRYER, WALTER. 'Bledlow migrants to the north', *Origins: magazine of the Buckinghamshire Family History Society* 7(3), 1983, 114-5. Extracts from 1851 census returns for Lancashire and Cheshire relating to migrants from this Buckinghamshire village.

Barnton

'1851 census for Barnton, Cheshire: index of surnames appearing', *F.H.S.C.J.* 4(2), 1973, 13-14.

Burton

'Surnames appearing in the 1851 census of Burton, Cheshire', *F.H.S.C.J.* 3(1), 1972, 3.

Caldy

'1851 census return, Caldy, Wirral: parish of West Kirby, household of Richard Barton,

jnr', *F.H.S.C.J.* 12(3), 1983, 9. Census return for a relatively small gentleman's household.

Chester Castle

TURNER, M. 'Anyone you know here?', *F.H.C.J.S.* 9(3) 1980, 19-25; 9(4) 1980, 11-15; 10(1), 1980, 5-14. Transcript of the 1851 census for Chester Castle, listing many soldiers, prisoners, *etc.*

Frodsham

'1851 census for Crosbie House Boarding School, Main Street, Frodsham, Cheshire', *F.H.S.C.J.* 10(2), 1980, 13-14.

Grange

JONES, HARTLEY. 'Township of Grange, parish of West Kirby, 1851 census', *F.H.S.C.J.* 10(4), 1981, 66-7; 11(1), 1981, 14.

Hoylake

'1851 census strays, Hoose Ward, Hoylake', *F.H.S.C.J.* 8(4), 1979, 21-2.

Knutsford

MAY, ERIC. '1851 census return for the House of Correction, Knutsford, Cheshire', *F.H.S.C.J.* 12(1), 1982, 8-10; 12(2), 1982, 10-14.

Newton

JONES, HARTLEY. '1851 census for township of Newton-cum-Larton, parish of West Kirby, Cheshire', *F.H.S.C.J.* 10(2), 1980, 7.

Oxton

LAMBERT, NORMAN. 'Cheshire 1851 census: Oxton, parish of Woodchurch', *F.H.S.C.J.* 13(1), 1983, 14-15. Extract only.

Poynton

'Poynton: the census and the enumerators', *Cheshire history* 17, 1986, 8-13. Analysis of 1851 census.

'The census and the enumerators', *Poynton Local History Society newsletter* 6, 1983, 3-24. Includes list of householder surnames in 1851 census for Poynton; also biographical notes on census enumerators, *etc.*

Puddington

'Surnames appearing in the 1851 census of Puddington, Cheshire', *F.H.S.C.J.* 3(1), 1972, 3.

Runcorn

'1851 census of Church Street, Runcorn, boarding and day schools', *F.H.S.C.J.* 6(1), 1976, 6.

South Halton

CAPENER, J.S.A. *A transcript of the 1851 census returns for the townships of Acton Grange, Aston by Sutton, Aston Grange, Clifton, Daresbury, Halton, Keckwick, Moore, Newton by Daresbury, Norton, Preston, Stockham, Sutton and Weston, with an index of surnames.* Halton historical publications 6. [Halton]: Halton Borough Council, 1987.

Tatton Hall

SANT, TONY. 'Tatton Hall, Cheshire in 1851', *N.C.F.H.* 15(4), 1988, 105. Census of Tatton Hall staff.

1861

Marple

SIMPSON, J. 'No Man's Land', *Manchester genealogist,* 16(4), 1980, 105. 1861 census for a street in Marple.

Puddington

CHORLEY, B.M. 'Surnames appearing in the 1861 census of Puddington, Cheshire', *F.H.S.C.J.* 3(1), 1972, 18.

1871

Boughton

'1871 census for the Certified Ragged and Industrial School, Boughton', *F.H.S.C.J.* 11(2), 1981, 8-11.

Chester

MAY, ERIC F. 'Chester Gaol: 1871 census return', *F.H.S.C.J.* 15(3), 1986, 7.
'1871 census: 1st Royal Cheshire Militia, Chester St. Mary, RG10 3724', *F.H.S.C.J.* 14(1), 1984, 10-11.
'1871 census for Chester (MF24/34; RG10/3224): Union Workhouse (Lower Bridge Street Girls School)', *F.H.S.C.J.* 15(2), 1985, 5.

Spital

'1871 census for Spital, Boughton, Chester (House of refuge)', *F.H.S.C.J.* 11(1), 1981, 10.

1881

1881 census of Cheshire: surname & location indexes. Northwich: F.H.S.C. 1988- . v.1. Northwich District: Northwich, Over, Middlewich & other townships. v.2-5. Altrincham District. All published to date.

Chester. St. Martin

MAY, E.F. '1881 census return: Militia Barracks, 1st Royal Cheshire Militia, St. Martins parish, Chester', *F.H.S.C.J.* 13(3), 1984, 7-8.

Hampton

MAY, ERIC. '[Extracts from the 1881 census for New Hall, Hampton, and Edge Hall, Edge]', *F.H.S.C.J.* 13(2), 1983, 9.

Poynton

KENDALL, GILLIAN, ed. 'Poynton in the 1881 census', *Poynton Local History Society newsletter* 12, 1986, 1-51. Includes list of surnames, and much analysis.

1891

LANGSTON, B., & MOILLIET, A. *1891 census of Cheshire, surname & address indexes: Northwich district, P.R.O. pieces RG12/2835 to 2842.* Northwich; F.H.S.C., Northwich Group, 1992.

F. *Census of Landowners.*

A different type of census was taken in 1873. Everyone who owned an acre or more of land is listed in:
'Chester', in *Return of owners of land, 1873.* House of Commons Parliamentary papers, LXXVII, 1874, 119-58. This covers the whole county.

9. DIRECTORIES, MAPS AND DIALECT

A. Directories.

Directories are invaluable sources for locating people in the nineteenth and early twentieth centuries; they are the equivalent of the modern phone book. Many directories for Cheshire were published. The following list is selective; further items may be identified by consulting the works listed in my *English Genealogy; an introductory guide*. In general, the many directories treating Cheshire and Lancashire together - and especially directories of the Manchester and Stockport region - are not listed here; for these, see: TUPLING, G.H. *Lancashire directories, 1684-1957*, rev. Sidney Horrocks. A contribution towards a Lancashire bibliography 1. Manchester: Joint Committee on the Lancashire Bibliography, 1968.

The list which follows is in rough chronological order.

BROSTER, PETER. *The Chester guide, or, an account of the ancient and present state of that city . . . to which is added a directory containing an alphabetical list of the clergy, merchants, tradesmen, &c., in the city and market towns in the county.* Chester: P. Broster, 1781-7. 3 issues. Subsequent issues have no directory. The 1781 edition has recently been published on microfiche, Chester: Cheshire County Council, 1994.

DYKE, ESTELLE. 'Chester's earliest directories, 1781 and 1782', *J.C.A.H.S.* N.S., 37(2), 1949, 243-93. New edition of the directory portions of Broster's *The Chester guide*, 1781 and 1782 editions.

TUNNICLIFF, WILLIAM. *A topographical survey of the Counties of Stafford, Chester and Lancaster . . .* Nantwich: E. Snelson, 1787. Includes directory of the principal merchants and manufacturers.

COWDROY, W. *The directory & guide for the city and county of Chester, with a concise history . . .* Chester: W. Cowdroy, 1789. Microfiche edition published Chester: Cheshire County Council, 1993.

Pigot and Co's national commercial directory . . . counties of Chester, Cumberland, Durham, Lancaster, Northumberland,

Westmoreland, and York . . . J. Pigot & Co., 1834. The Cheshire portion has been reprinted as *Pigot and Co's commercial directory for the County of Cheshire, 1834.* Swinton: Neil Richardson, 1982.

A directory of the towns and principal villages throughout the extensive manufacturing district round Manchester, with a selection of other towns in Cheshire and Lancashire and the whole of North Wales, the entire forming a valuable supplement to the last Manchester directory. Manchester: I. Slater, 1844.

BAGSHAW, SAMUEL. *History, gazetteer and directory of the County Palatine of Chester . . .* Sheffield: Samuel Bagshaw, 1850. Microfiche ed. published Chester: Cheshire County Council, 1993.

A new alphabetical and classified directory of Chester . . . Manchester: Wm. Whellan, 1854. In fact covers most of Cheshire.

Slater's royal national commercial directory of the northern counties. Vol.2: Cheshire, Cumberland, Lancashire and Westmoreland. Manchester: I. Slater, 1855.

Post Office directory of Cheshire. Kelly & Co., 1857-78. Continued by: *Kelly's directory of Cheshire.* 1892-1939. Many issues. 1857, 1865, 1892 and 1896 volumes reprinted on microfiche, Chester: Cheshire County Council, 1993-4.

History gazetteer and directory of Cheshire, comprising a general survey of the county . . . Sheffield: F. White & Co., 1860. Microfiche edition, Chester: Cheshire County Council, 1994.

Morris & Co's directory & gazetteer of Cheshire. Nottingham: Morris & Co., 1864-74. 2 editions; title varies. Microfiche of both editions published Chester: Cheshire County Council, 1993-4.

Slater's royal national commercial directory of Cheshire, with a classified trades directory of Liverpool, with topographical notices of each city, town and village . . . Manchester: Isaac Slater, 1869-90. 4 issues. Title varies. All volumes reprinted on microfiche, Chester: Cheshire County Council, 1994.

Bennett's business dirctory for Cheshire. Birmingham: Bennett & Co., 1903.

Cheshire directory and buyers guide, 1909. Walsall. E.F. Cope & Co., 1909-35. 6 issues.

Cheshire directory. Walsall: Aubrey & Co., 1933-40. Annual.

Alderley
THOMPSON, HARGREAVES. *Alderley, Alderley Edge, Wilmslow, Styal and Handforth directory.* Manchester: Isaac Slater, 1888.

Altrincham
BALSHAW, CHARLES. *Charles Balshaw's stranger's guide and complete directory to Altrincham, Bowdon, Dunham, Timperley, Baguley, Ashley, Hale & Bollington.* Altrincham: Charles Balshaw, 1855-9. 3 issues. 1854/5 issue reprinted Didsbury: E.J. Marten, 1973.

THOMPSON, HARGREAVES, et al. *Altrincham, Bowdon, Dunham Massey, Hale, Timperley & Ashley directory.* Manchester: T. & R. Percy, 1886.

Slater's directory of Altrincham, Bowdon, Sale, Brooklands, and Dunham Massey, and neighbourhood . . . Manchester: Slater's Directory, 1901-2.

Birkenhead
Mortimer and Harwood's directory of Birkenhead. Birkenhead: Wm. Osborne, 1843.

Caldy
Directory: Caldy, Great Meols, Hoylake and West Kirby. West Kirby: C. Hawling & Co., 1922.

Chester
The Chester general directory. Chester: Parry and Son, 1840.

Williams's commercial directory of the city and borough of Chester . . . Liverpool: J. Williams, 1846.

Phillipson & Golder's directory for Chester and the immediate neighbourhood . . . Chester: Phillipson & Golder, 1870-1936. Almost annual. Title varies.

Slater's Post Office directory of the City of Chester and its suburbs. Manchester: Isaac Slater, 1882-8. 3 issues; title varies.

Kelly's directory of Chester and neighbourhood, including Great Boughton, Hoole, and Upton (incorporating Phillipson & Golder's directory of Chester and its immediate neighbourhood). Kelly's directories, 1936-74. 20 issues. Title varies.

Crewe
PORTER, FRANK. *Postal directory for Crewe, Middlewich, Nantwich, Sandbach, Northwich, Winsford, and district, containing street, classified, trade, & commercial lists.* Liverpool: Rockliffe Bros., 1889.

Postal directory for Crewe, Congleton, Middlewich, Nantwich, Northwich, Sandbach, Winsford, Wybunbury, Holmes Chapel, Wrenbury and Alsager with the villages intervening . . . Hanley: Staffordshire Sentinel, 1913.

Hoylake
Hoylake and West Kirby directory: a complete list of residents, churches and chapels, institutions, clubs, schools, &c., in the Urban District of Hoylake and West Kirby, with annals of the district from the earliest historical records to the present time. Hoylake: Gill & Co., 1897.

MOSS JOHN. *Moss's directory of Hoylake and West Kirby.* West Kirby: John Moss, 1906.

Macclesfield
CORRY, JOHN. *The history of Macclesfield.* J. Fergusson, 1817. Includes 'a list of the manufacturers, tradesmen &c. of Macclesfield in 1817'; also pollbook, 1804.

The history and directory of Macclesfield. Manchester: W.D.Varey, 1825. Includes monumental inscriptions.

Slater's directory of Macclesfield and District, with a list of the gentry and alphabetical, classified trades, and street directories . . . Manchester: Isaac Slater, 1887-90. 2 issues.

The Macclesfield and District directory, including the following: Alderley Edge, Bollington, Bramhall, Congleton, Wilmslow, and the numerous townships and villages in the surrounding districts. Macclesfield: Heath Bros., 1924.

Malpas
HAYNS, DAVID. 'Sources for Malpas history, 1: local directories', *Malpas history* 6, 1986, 19-28. Includes extracts from an 1890 directory.

Poynton
SHERCLIFF, W.H. 'Poynton in directories', *Cheshire history* 5, 1980, 57-68. General discussion of entries in directories relating to Poynton.

Stockport

William's commercial directory of Stockport, Preston, Wigan, &c., &c. Manchester: J. Williams, 1845.

Slater's classified commercial directory of the towns and villages in the extensive manufacturing district round Manchester, forming an appropriate and valuable companion to the Manchester and Salford directory. Manchester: issue Slater, 1851. Includes Stockport, Altrincham, *etc.*

Worrall's directory of Stockport, Heaton Norris, Macclesfield, Congleton, Hyde, Denton, Marple, Glossop, New Mills, Buxton, Chapel en le Frith, Hayfield, Whaley Bridge and adjoining townships, with a list of the silk throwsters and manufacturers in Leek. Oldham: J. Worrall, 1872.

Slater's Royal national commercial directory of Stockport, Heaton Norris and district. Manchester: Isaac Slater, 1887-93. 3 issues.

Wood's directory of Stockport, 1887. Manchester: Edward B. Woods, 1887-99. 2 issues.

Kelly's directory of Manchester and Salford, with suburbs and Stockport. Kelly & Co., 1891.

The Stockport directory. Stockport: New Cheshire Country News Co., 1899-1910. 5 issues. Title varies; 1907 and 1910 issues add *and Hazel Grove.*

B. *Gazetteers and Maps.*

The parishes of Cheshire are frequently large and contain many separate townships. Prestbury, for example, has no less than 38! In these circumstances, a good gazetteer of the county is needed in order to locate particular places. This is provided by:

DUNN, F.I. *The ancient parishes, townships and chapelries of Cheshire.* Chester: Cheshire Record Office, 1987.

An even more detailed guide to Cheshire place-names is:

DODGSON, J. McN. *The place-names of Cheshire.* English Place-Name Society **44-8** & **54**. 1970-81. Pt.1. County names, regional and forest names, river names, road names, the place-names of Macclesfield Hundred. Pt.2. The place-names of Bucklow Hundred and Northwich Hundred. Pt.3. The place-names of Nantwich Hundred and Eddisbury Hundred. Pt.4. The place-names of Broxton Hundred and Wirral Hundred. Pt.5(1) The place-names of the city of Chester. The elements of Cheshire place-names, A-Gylden. Pt.5(2). The elements of Cheshire place-names, Haca-Yolden. Analysis of fieldname types. The personal names in Cheshire place-names. To be continued.

See also:

A Cheshire index. 2nd ed. corrected. Chester: County Health Dept., 1968. Gazetteer, listing inhabited places, intended for the use of health workers, but also useful to genealogists. A 3rd edition was published 1973, but relates to the county after the 1974 boundary changes.

BROWN, W.E. 'Notes on Chester street names past and present', *J.C.A.H.S.* N.S., **13**, 1906, 53-66.

HASWELL, GEORGE W. 'Notes on Chester street-names past and present (northern section)', *J.C.A.H.S.* N.S., **13**, 1906, 26-52. Locates place names no longer used.

These gazetteers may be complemented by historic maps of the county. A comprehensive listing of them is to be found in:

WHITAKER, HAROLD. *A descriptive list of the printed maps of Cheshire, 1577-1900.* Cm.S., N.S., **106**. 1942.

See also:

HARLEY, J.B. 'From Saxton to Speed', *Cheshire round* 1(6), 1966, 174-84.

HARLEY, J.B. 'Ogilby and Collins', *Cheshire round* 1(7), 210-25.

HARLEY, J.B. 'Maps of early Georgian Cheshire', *Cheshire round* 1(8), 1967, 256-69.

HARLEY, J.B. 'Cheshire maps, 1787-1831', *Cheshire round* 1(9), 1968, 290-305.

HARRISON, W. 'Early maps of Cheshire', *H.S.L.C.* **26**, 1909, 1-26.

TOOLEY, R.V. 'Large scale English county maps and plans of cities not printed in atlases, part 5: Cheshire', *Map collector* **17**, 1981, 22-66. List.

SKILLERN, WILLIAM J. *Cheshire maps in the Stockport local history collection.* Handlist 3. Stockport: Stockport Public Libraries, 1962. There are a number of facsimile editions of historic maps which are readily available:

BURDETT, P.P. *A survey of the County Palatine of Chester: P.B.Burdett, 1777,* ed. J.B. Harley & P. Laxton. Occasional series 1. Widnes: Historic Society of Lancashire and Cheshire, 1974. Map.

SYLVESTER, DOROTHY & NULTY, GEOFFREY, eds.
The historical atlas of Cheshire. Chester:
Cheshire Community Council, 1958. Maps
illustrating the history of Cheshire, with
commentaries.
*The village atlas: the growth of Manchester,
Lancashire and North Cheshire, 1840-1912.*
Edmonton: Alderman Press, 1989. Facsimiles
of contemporary maps.
*The old series Ordnance Survey maps of
England and Wales . . . volume VII: North-
Central England . . .* Lympne Castle: Harry
Margary, 1989.

C. *Dialect.*

Dialect words frequently occur in genealogical
source material and may cause confusion. A
number of glossaries are available to put you
right:
DARLINGTON, THOMAS. *The folk-speech of
South Cheshire.* English Dialect Society,
1887.
HOLLAND, ROBERT. *A glossary of words used
in the County of Chester.* English Dialect
Society, 1886.
LEIGH, EGERTON. *A glossary of words used in
the dialect of Cheshire.* Wakefield: E.P.
Publishing, 1973. Originally published 1877.
WRIGHT, PETER. *The Cheshire chatterer: how it
is spoke.* [ ]: Dalesman Books, 1974.

10. ESTATE AND FAMILY PAPERS

A. *General*

The records of estate administration - deeds,
leases, rentals, surveys, accounts, *etc.* - are a
mine of information for the genealogist. Many
of these records have been printed in full or
in part, although much more still lies
untouched in the archives. The plea rolls of the
Palatinate of Chester record innumerable land
transactions; they are calendared in:
TURNER, PETER. 'Welsh records: calendar of
deeds, inquisitions and writs of dower
enrolled on the plea rolls of the County of
Chester', *Twenty-sixth annual report of the
Deputy Keeper of the Public Records,*
1865, appendix, 36-55; *Twenty-seventh . . .,*
1866, appendix, 94-123; *Twenty-eighth . . .,*
1867, appendix, 20-71; *Twenty-ninth . . .,*
1868, appendix, 49-98; *Thirtieth . . .,* 1868,
appendix, 121-65. 13-16th c.
The 'feet of fines' held in the Public Record
Office, constitute one of the major collections
of deeds for pre-industrial England. They have
not, unfortunately, been fully calendared for
Cheshire; see, however:
RHODES, E.H. 'No. 5: Welsh records. Calendar
of fines, counties of Chester and Flint,
Edward I, removed from Chester to the
Public Record Office in 1854', *Twenty-eighth
annual report of the Deputy Keeper of the
Public Records,* 1867, 6-19.
B., J. 'Cheshire fines', *C.Sf.* 3rd series **17**, 1922,
25-55, *passim.* List of feet of fines for
1625-6.
'Chester fines and recoveries', *C.Sf.* 3rd series
12, 1917, 74-90, *passim.* Calendar of deeds,
1767.
A major collection of deeds, including many
from Cheshire, is held in the John Rylands
Library of the University of Manchester. See:
TYSON, MOSES. 'Hand-list of charters, deeds and
similar documents in the possession of the
John Rylands Library, II(3): documents
acquired from various sources', *Bulletin of
the John Rylands Library* **18**, 1934, 393-454.
Lists much Cheshire and Lancashire
material, but also documents from various
other counties. See also section 2B above
Cheshire Record Office also holds many
collections of family and estate papers. A brief
note on these, including a summary list of the

Cholmondeley of Cholmondeley archives is printed in:
'Private collection', *F.H.S.C.J.* **3**(2), 1972, 6.
For an important collection of abstracts from early Cheshire charters, see:
BARRACLOUGH, GEOFFREY. *Facsimiles of early Cheshire charters.* Oxford: Basil Blackwell, 1957.
Other general works on Cheshire deeds *etc.* include:
CLAYTON, DOROTHY. 'An early Cheshire archivist, Faithful Thomas (c. 1772-1844) and the records of the Palatinate of Chester', *Archives* 17(76), 1986, 3-26. Includes a list of the calendars he compiled.
PHILLIPS, CINDY. 'Title deeds index', *N.C.F.H.* **20**(4), 1993, 106. Brief discussion of an index to a collection of deeds dating from 1709.
STEWART-BROWN, R. 'Early Cheshire deeds', *C.Sf.* 3rd series **19**, 1924, 15-28, *passim.* Brief abstracts of 24 medieval deeds, from notes made for the heraldic visitation of 1580.

B. *Ecclesiastical estates and chartularies, etc.*

In the medieval period, a great deal of property was owned by ecclesiastical institutions such as churches, monasteries, dioceses, *etc.* For the estates of the Diocese of Chester, see:
FISHWICK, HENRY, ed. *Lancashire & Cheshire church surveys, 1649-1655.* L.C.R.S. 1. 1879. Pt.1. Parochial surveys of Lancashire. Pt.2. Surveys of the lands, &c., of the Bishop and Dean and Chapter of Chester, and of the warden and fellows of the Collegiate church of Manchester.

Birkenhead Priory
'Rental of Birkenhead Priory at the Dissolution', *Wirral notes and queries* **2**, 1893, 39 & 43.

Chester. St. Anne
BENNETT, J.H.E. 'St Anne's, Chester', *C.Sf.* 3rd series **5**, 1904, 19-20 & 24. Rental of the hospital, 1622.
B[ENNETT]. J.H.E. 'Chartulary of the Hospital of St. Anne, Chester', *C.Sf.* 3rd series **36**, 1948, *passim.*

Chester, St. Mary's Nunnery
IRVINE, WM.FERGUSSON. 'Notes on the history of St. Mary's Nunnery, Chester', *J.C.A.H.S.* N.S., **13**, 1906, 67-109. Includes abstracts of deeds, and a rental of 1526, naming tenants in Chester.

Chester. St. Werburgh
TAIT, JAMES, ed. *The chartulary or register of the Abbey of St. Werburgh, Chester.* Cm.S., N.S. 79 & 82. 1920-23. Includes list of bishops, abbots, earls and justices of Chester, medieval.
McCONNELL, E.K. 'The Abbey of St. Werburgh, Chester, in the thirteenth century', *H.S.L.C.* **55-6**; N.S., **19-20**, 1903-4, 42-66. Includes deeds, pleas, *etc.*
BIRCH, W.DE GRAY. 'On some manuscripts relating to St. Werburgh's Abbey, Chester, preserved in the British Museum', *J.C.A.H.S.* N.S., **3**, 1890, 1-25.

Vale Royal Abbey
BROWNBILL, JOHN, ed. *The ledger book of Vale Royal Abbey.* L.C.R.S. **68**. 1914. Includes biographical notes on abbots.

Yeaveley
B[ENNETT], J.H.E. 'The fraternity of Yeaveley', *C.Sf.* 3rd series **12**, 1917, 78-9. Medieval rental of the lands of the Order of St. John of Jerusalem.

C. *Local estate records*

Many estate papers relating to particular places are in print; these are listed here, together with a few works based on local estate records.

Aldford
B., J. 'The homagers of Aldford', *C.Sf.* 3rd series **22**, 1927, 32-3. Lists men owing homage, 1345.

Bebington
I[RVINE], W.F. 'Some early Bebington charters', *C.Sf.* 3rd series **47**, 1953, 31-610 *passim;* **48**, 1956, 2-12, *passim.* Medieval.

Bickley
A., F.S. 'Sir Hugh Cholmondeley's muster roll, 1570', *C.Sf.* 3rd series **19**, 1924, 84-93, *passim.* Muster of tenants at Bickley and Hetherston.

Birkenhead

D., J. 'An old Birkenhead rental', *C.Sf.* 3rd series 21 1926, 83-4. Early 18th c.

Blacon

'The manor of Blacon', *C.Sf.* 3rd series 21, 1926, 93. Rental, 1679.

Bramhall

CLEMESHA, H.W. 'The new court book of the manor of Bramhall, (1632-1657)', *Chetham miscellanies* N.S., 4. Cm.S., N.S., 80. 1921. Separately paginated.

Brimstage

'Rent roll of Brimstage in 1557', *Wirral notes and queries* 2, 1893, 5-6.

Burton

CULLEN, MARGARET. 'The manor court of Burton and its records', *Burton and District Local History Society bulletin* 1, 1977, 6-7. 16-18th c.

Caldy

WILTSHIRE, PERSIS. 'Manorial records of Caldy', *F.H.S.C.J.* 15(1), 1985, 9-10. Lists tenants, mid-18th c.

Chester

STEWART-BROWN, R. 'Some early Chester deeds', *C.Sf.* 3rd series 17, 1922, 93-7, *passim.* Abstracts of 34 medieval deeds.

TAYLOR, HENRY. 'Notes upon some early deeds relating to Chester and Flint', *J.C.A.H.S.* N.S., 2, 1888, 149-85.

STEWART-BROWN, R. *The Domesday roll of Chester: some 13th century enrolments.* Chester: Courant Press, 1924. Deed abstracts.

STEWART-BROWN, R. 'The Domesday roll of Chester', *C.Sf.* 3rd series 20, 1924, *passim.* 13th c. deed abstracts *etc.*

TAYLOR, HENRY. 'Six thirteenth century Chester deeds', *C.Sf.* 3rd series 13, 1918, 5-6.

TAYLOR, HENRY. 'Ten early Chester deeds, 1270-1490', *J.C.A.H.S.* N.S., 10, 1903, 101-16.

IRVINE, WM. FERGUSSON. 'Early deeds from Aston Hall, relating to Chester', *C.Sf.* 3rd series 28, 1935, 59-95, *passim;* 29, 1935, *passim;* 31, 1937, *passim.* 14-15th c.

FRAGEOCRA. 'Lands in Chester in 14th century', *C.Sf.* 3rd series 56, 1963, 73-97, *passim.* Deed abstracts.

B[ENNETT], J.H.E. 'Old leases of Chester city lands', *C.Sf.* 3rd series 19, 1923, *passim.* Abstracts of leases, 1356-1775.

B[ENNETT], J.H.E. 'Gable rents of Chester', *C.Sf.* 3rd series 26, 1934, 70-83, *passim.* See also 32, 1938, 67-88, *passim.* Lists Chester tenants liable to certain customary duties, 1533-4.

B[ENNETT,] J.H.E. 'The Fraternity of St. George, Chester', *C.Sf.* 3rd series 21, 1926, 62-3. Rental, 1622.

B., J. 'Lease of former church property', *C.Sf.* 3rd series 10, 1914, 61. Lists tenants of lands formerly belonging to St. John's church, Chester, in 1595.

B[ENNETT], J.H.E. 'Five deeds relating to Bridge Street, Foregate Street, and Castle Lane, Chester, *C.Sf.* 3rd series 23, 1928, 49-50.

MONTGOMERY, R. MORTIMER. 'Some early deeds relating to land on the north side of Eastgate Street, Chester', *J.C.A.H.S.* N.S., 22, 1915-16, 117-41. Discussion of Aldersey family deeds.

'Deeds relating to property in Foregate Street, Chester', *C.Sf.* series 29, 1935, 41-7. 17-18th c.

TAYLOR, HENRY. 'Six early deeds relating to property in Northgate Street, Chester', *J.C.A.H.S.* 6(1), 1897, 49-59.

B[ENNETT], J.H.E. 'Deeds relating to Northgate Street property', *C.Sf.* 3rd series 35, 1948, 12-13. 14-16th c.

'Leche property in Pepper Street, Chester *C.Sf.* 3rd series 49, 1956, 31-47, *passim.* Deed abstracts *etc.,* 17th c.

B[ENNETT], J.H.E. 'St. John's House, Chester', *C.Sf.* 3rd series 31, 1937, 70-110. Abstract of title deeds, 17-19th c.

B[ENNETT], J.H.E. 'Property in Watergate Street, Chester', *C.Sf.* 3rd series 31, 1937, 79. Deeds, 17-18th c.

B[ENNETT] J.H.E. 'Six deeds relating to property in Watergate Street, Chester', *C.Sf.* 3rd series 17, 1922, 70-71. 16-19th c.

B[ENNETT], J.H.E. 'A catalogue of Aldersey deeds', *C.Sf.* 3rd series 26, 1934, 33-63, *passim.* Mainly relating to Chester.

TAYLOR, A. HENRY. 'A transcript of old Chester deeds', *J.C.A.H.S.* N.S., 5(4), 1895, 427-32. Medieval deeds relating to the Doncaster family.

IRVINE, WM. FERGUSSON. 'Chester in the twelfth and thirteenth centuries, being notes on a number of recently discovered documents relating to the city, dating from the year 1178', *J.C.A.H.S.* N.S., **10**, 1903, 13-53. Abstracts of 73 deeds of the Erneys family.

MORTON, T.N. 'The family of Moore of Liverpool; rough list of their paper records', *H.S.L.C.* **38**, N.S., **2**, 1886, 149-58. Estate papers relating to Liverpool, Kirkdale, *etc.* in Lancashire, and to Chester and the Wirral.

B[ENNETT], J.H.E. 'Moore rentals of Cheshire property', *C.Sf.* 3rd series **22**, 1927, 42, 43-4, & 45-6. Rentals for Chester property of Moore of Bank Hall, Lancashire, c. 1480 and c. 1540.

S[TEWART-B[ROWN], R. 'Rental of the Chester property of William Moore of Bank Hall, circa 1540', *C.Sf.* 3rd series **11**, 1915, 1.

B[ENNETT], J.H.E. 'Chester possessions of the Norris family', *C.Sf.* 3rd series **47**, 1953, 10-45. Notes from rentals of 1468 and 1488 *etc.*

'An old Cheshire rental', *C.Sf.* 3rd series **5**, 1904, 103-4. Speke family rental for Chester, mid-15th c.

Church Lawton

RENAUD, FRANK. Church Lawton manor records', *L.C.A.S.* **5**, 1887, 19-63. Extracts, medieval-17th c.

Claughton

IRVINE, WM. FERGUSSON. 'A court roll of the manor of Cloughton, 1689', *Wirral notes and queries* **2**, 1893, 55-6.

Coddington

STEWART-BROWN, R. 'Coddington deeds', *C.Sf.* 3rd series **18**, 1923, 41-8, *passim.* Abstracts of 46 medieval deeds.

Combermere

'Combermere deeds', *C.Sf.* 3rd series **28, 33, 37-9, 49** & **50**, 1935-58, *passim.* Abstracts from a 17th c. cartulary relating to Combermere.

Crabhall

See Great Saughall

Dukinfield

'Rent roll of Dukinfield in 1717', *A.N.Q.* **2**, 1883, 99.

Dunham on the Hill

BENNETT], J.H.E. 'Some deeds relating to Dunham on the Hill', *C.Sf.* 3rd series **13**, 1918, 46-7. 15th c.

PORTER, G.E. 'The value of farm notebooks: a new example from Cheshire', *Local historian* **13**, 1979, 270-76. Brief discussion of the notebook of John Byram of Eastham, 1839-71.

Great Saughall

'Fragment of a rental for 1563 relating to Great and Little Saughall, Crabhall, Poulton *cum* Seacombe, and Liscard', *C.Sf.* 3rd series **23**, 1928, 78-9 & 80-81.

Halton

BEAMONT, W. *An account of the rolls of the Honour of Halton, part of Her Majesty the Queen's Duchy of Lancaster, being the substance of a report recently made upon the removal of the records from Halton Castle in Cheshire, to the office of the public records, London.* Warrington: Percival Pearse, 1897.

'Old grants of land in Halton, Hatton and New Newton *juxta* Daresbury', *C.Sf.* 3rd series **23**, 1928. 11-14, *passim.* Medieval deeds.

Handbridge

B[EAZLEY], F.C. 'Handbridge court roll, 1734', *C.Sf.* 3rd series **8**, 1911, 81 & 85-6. Transcript; many names.

Hetherston

See Bickley

Hoose

'The court roll of the manor of Hoose in 1812', *C.Sf.* 3rd series **2** 1896, 140-41.

Hotten

See Halton

Hooton

'The court baron of the manor of Hooton, 1698', *C.Sf.* 3rd series **51**, 1956, 44-66.

Ince

HOLLY. 'The rental of St. Werburgh's Abbey in the township of Ince, 1398', *C.Sf.* 3rd series **24**, 1929, 33-5, *passim.*

Irby

S[TEWART]-B[ROWN], R. 'Court rolls of Irby and Greasby', *C.Sf.* 3rd series **7**, 1910, 36. Brief list, 17-19th c.

Kinderton
See Middlewich

Knutsford
RYLANDS. W. HARRY. 'Deeds relating to Knutsford, Co. Chester', *H.S.L.C.* **35**, 1883, 27-36. Abstracts, 17th c.

Liscard
WOODS, E. CUTHBERT. 'The journal of John Hough, lord of the manor of Liscard', *H.S.L.C.* **72**; N.S., **36**, 1920, 27-49. Includes many extracts, 18th c., concerning the manor; also pedigrees of Meoles and Hough, 17-18th c., Penkett, 18-19th c., and Maddock, 16-19th c. See also Great Saughall

Little Caldy
IRVINE, WM. FERGUSSON. 'The manor of Little Caldy in Wirral in 1453-4', *C.Sf.* 3rd series **5**, 1904, 35-7, 46-8, & 54-6. Includes rental, 1453-4.

Little Neston
'Deeds relating to Little Neston', *C.Sf.* 3rd series **27**, 1934, 53-79, *passim*. 17-18th c., includes pedigree of Cottingham.

Little Saughall
See Great Saughall

Longdendale
BOOTH, P.H.W. & HARRP, S.A. 'Extent of Longdendale, 1360', *C.Sf.* 5th series **1-106** & **107-191**, 1976, 8. *passim*.

Lower Bebington
'Court rolls of the manors of Lower Bebington and Poulton Lancelyn, 1380 to 1504', *C.Sf.* 3rd series **15**, 1920, 36-7. 39 & 45. Brief extract.

Lymm
THOMAS, G.H. 'Eighteenth century enclosure in Lymm', *J.L.D.L.H.S.* **2**(2), 1986, 2-8. Includes list of proprietors, 1765.

Macclesfield
CURRY, ANNE. 'The court rolls of the Lordship of Macclesfield, 1345-1485', *Cheshire history* **12**, 1983, 5-10. General discussion, listing the rolls.

HULLEY, R. 'Macclesfield court rolls, 1369-1370', *N.C.F.H.* **21**(1), 1993, 33. Brief notes on a manuscript index.

Middlewich
VARLEY, JOAN, ed. *A Middlewich chartulary compiled by William Vernon in the seventeenth century.* Cm.S., N.S., **105** & **108**. 1941-4. v.2. edited jointly with James Tait. 'Middlewich and Kinderton deeds', *C.Sf.* 3rd series **10**, 1914, *passim*. Medieval-17th c. deeds of the Venables, Vernon and other families.

Minshull Vernon
RENAUD, FRANK. 'Deeds relating to early tenures of land, &c., in Minshull Vernon and adjacent townships in Cheshire', *L.C.A.S.* **15**, 1897, 49-62. Abstracts.

Nantwich
HALL, JAMES, ed. 'The book of the abbot of Combermere, 1289 to 1529', in *Miscellanies relating to Lancaster and Cheshire* **2**. L.C.R.S. **31**. 1896. Separately paginated. Deeds, leases, and rentals relating to Nantwich, 1385-1526.

Newhall
'The manor of Newhall in 1609', *C.Sf.* 3rd series **39**, 1948. 63-83, *passim*. Survey, listing tenants.

Newton
HALL, JAMES. 'A court roll and a court summons for Newton and Sutton, near Middlewich', *C.Sf.* N.S., **1**, 1895, 40-42. 1640. See also Halton

Northenden
See Yeardsley

Northwich
See Yeardsley

Oakhanger Moss
DUCKWOOD. 'Turbary and firebote', *C.Sf.* 3rd series **4**, 1903, 103-4. 'Mosse bouke', listing persons who paid for 'Turbary and firebote' in Oakhanger Moss.

Over Whitley
S[TEWART]-B[ROWN], R. 'Over Whitley halmotes',
C.Sf. 3rd series **11**, 1915, 89-90. Lists tenants
in 1529.

Poulton
See Great Saughall

Poulton Lancelyn
See Lower Bebington

Poynton
SHERCLIFF, W.H. 'Three surveys of Poynton,
1770, 1793 and 1849', *Poynton Local History
Society newsletter* **8**, 1984, 11-24. Includes
lists of tenants.

Preston on the Hill
'Deeds relating to Preston on the Hill', *C.Sf.*
3rd series **27**, 1934, 42-9, *passim.* 15-18th c.

Saighton
HOLLY. A sixteenth century boundary deed of
Saighton', *C.Sf.* 3rd series **24**, 1929, 37-8.
Includes list of leases.

Sandbach
B., J. 'Sandbach court roll, 1589', *C.Sf.* 3rd series
10, 1913, 2, 3-4, 6 & 8.

Seccombe
See Great Saughall

Stalybridge
STEWART-BROWN, R. 'Stalybridge and the
Staveley family', *C.Sf.* 3rd series **18**, 1923, 21,
24 & 26. Abstracts of 38 medieval deeds.

Stockport
TAYLOR, W.M.P. *A history of the Stockport
court leet.* Publication 3. Stockport:
Stockport Museum, 1971. Includes records of
the leets for 1663 and 1835.
'Terrier for Stockport, 1663', *C.Sf.* 3rd series
59, 1965, 6972, *passim.* Includes rental,
listing tenants.
GILES, PHYLLIS, M. 'The enclosure of common
lands in Stockport', *L.C.A.S.* **62**, 1950-51, 73-
110. Includes list of land purchasers, 1805.
'Stockport common lands', *A.N.Q.* **1**, 1882, 123-
4. See also 97 & 119-20. Lists purchasers,
early 19th c.

Sutton
See Newton

Tarporley
B., R. 'Manor court of Tarporley', *C.Sf.* 3rd
series **49**, 1956, 66-7. Abstract of proceedings,
1810.

Tarvin
'Survey of the manor of Tarvin in 1298', *C.Sf.*
3rd series **50**, 1958, 22-7, *passim.*

Tatton
'Leases for lives', *N.C.F.H.* 16(3), 1989, 93-5;
16(4), 1989, 125-7. List of 54 leases in the
manor of Tatton, 16-17th c., naming lessees
and 'lives'.

Wallasey
I[RVINE], W.F. 'Thirteenth century charters
relating to Wallasey', *C.Sf.* 3rd series **43**,
1949, 15-17, *passim.*

Willaston
'The manor of Willaston in Wirral', *C.Sf.* 3rd
series **52**, 1957, 31-7, *passim.* Court roll, 1746.

Winnington
See Yeardsley

Wirral
BOOTH, JENNIFER E. 'A Wirral account book
and notary's register', *H.S.L.C.* 118, 1966,
77-85. Kept by John Glegg of Irby; general
description.
'Rental of the Earl of Derby's property in
Wirral, 1521-2', *C.Sf.* 3rd series **4**, 1903, 23-5,
36-7, 44-5 & 49-50.
IRVINE, WM. FERGUSSON. 'Muster roll of Mr.
Hough's tenantry in Wirral, 1590', *Wirral
notes and queries* **1**, 1892, 75-6.
See also Chester

Wybunbury
'Extracts from the Royalist Composition papers
for Cheshire: Sir Thomas Smith, of the city
of Chester, Knt, and Thomas Smith, his son
and heir-apparent', *C.Sf.* 3rd series **1**, 1896,
70-72, 9092, 93-5 & 96-7. Includes rental of
lands in Wybunbury 1646, listing many
tenants.

Yeardsley

STEWART-BROWN, R. 'Some East Cheshire deeds', *C.Sf.* 3rd series **24**, 1929, 39-46, *passim.* Abstracts of deeds relating to the Jodrell family, concerning Yeardsley; also Winnington and Northwich deeds, and Tatton family deeds concerning Northenden; medieval.

D. *Private estates*

Many families have preserved deeds and papers relating to their estates and private lives. Publications listing these papers, or based on them, are listed here where they refer to more than one or two localities.

Antrobus

HORWOOD, ALFRED J. 'The manuscripts of J.C. Antrobus, esq., of Eaton Hall, Cheshire', in HISTORICAL MANUSCRIPTS COMMISSION. *Second report . . .* C441. H.M.S.O., 1874, 69. Brief description of deeds *etc.,* relating to Cheshire, and also to Horton, Staffordshire.

Barnston

D., J.C.W. 'Early deeds of the Barnston family', *C.Sf.* 3rd series **42-3 & 49-50**, 1949-58, *passim.* Medieval-17th c.

Bradshaw

GIBSON, A. CRAIG. 'Every-day life of a country gentleman of Cheshire in the 17th century: as shewn in the private expenditure journal of Colonel Henry Bradshaw of Marple and Wybersleigh', *H.S.L.C.* **15**; N.S., **3**, 1863, 67-92. Includes transcript of accounts for 1640; many names.

Brereton

IVES, E.W., ed. *Letters and accounts of William Brereton of Malpas.* L.C.R.S. **116**. 1976. Estate papers.

'The families of Brereton and Carden, of Shocklach, Carden, and Wrexham *C.Sf.* 3rd series **27**, 1934, 4-9, *passim.* Medieval deeds.

Carden

See Brereton

Cholmondeley

'Cholmondeley deeds', *C.Sf.* 3rd series **53-4 & 56**, 1958-63, *passim.* Calendar; medieval.

Egerton

'Ellesmere collection', in *Guide to British historical manuscripts in the Huntington Library.* San Marino: Henry E. Huntington Library and Art Gallery, 1982, 21-77. Egerton family papers, 12-18th c., properties included lands in Cheshire and many other counties.

Egerton-Warburton

BEAMONT WILLIAM. *Arley charters: a calendar of ancient family charters preserved at Arley Hall, Cheshire, the seat of R.E. Egerton-Warburton, esquire, with notes and an explanatory introduction.* McCorquodale and Co., 1866.

Grey-Egerton

HORWOOD, ALFRED J. 'The manuscripts of Sir Philip de Malpas Grey-Egerton, Bart., M.P., of Oulton Hall, Co. Chester', in HISTORICAL MANUSCRIPTS COMMISSION. *Third report . . .* C.673, H.M.S.O., 1872, 244-46. Mainly 17th c. letters relating to public affairs; also brief summary of medieval deeds relating to Upton, Newton Hoole, and Bache.

Hardware

I[RVINE], W.F. 'The rental of Henry Hardware of the Peel in Mouldsworth, 1610', *C.Sf.,* 3rd series **29**, 1925, 65-70, *passim.* Rental listing tenants in Chester, Mouldsworth, *etc.*

Hatton Wood

TAYLOR, F. 'The Hatton Wood manuscripts in the John Rylands Library', *Bulletin of the John Rylands Library* **24**, 1940, 353-75. General description of a collection of deeds relating to Cheshire and many other counties.

Hoton

TAYLOR, HENRY. 'On some early deeds relating to the families of Hoton of Hooton, and Stanley of Storeton and Hooton', *J.C.A.H.S.* N.S., **6**(2), 1899, 167-216. Includes abstracts of 13 medieval deeds.

Lacy

LYONS, P.A., ed. *Two compoti of the Lancashire and Cheshire manors of Henry de Lacy, Earl of Lincoln, XXIV and XXXIII Edward I.* Cm.S., O.S., **112**. 1884.

Lathom

'Family of Lathom', *Journal of the British Archaeological Association* **7**, 1851, 415-70. Medieval deeds.

Legh

EARWAKER, J.P. 'The ancient charters and deeds at High Legh, Cheshire, belonging to Lt. Col. H. Cornwall Legh', *J.C.A.H.S.* N.S., 1, 1887, 1-29.

EARWAKER, J.P. 'Notes on the collection of deeds preserved at the East Hall, High Legh, Cheshire, with special reference to those relating to Manchester and the neighbourhood', *L.C.A.S.* 5, 1887, 259-71.

EARWAKER, J.P. 'Ancient Cheshire deeds', *C.N.Q.* 7, 1887, 68-70. Describes the Legh of High Legh archives.

TAYLOR, F. 'Hand-list of the Legh of Booths charters in the John Rylands Library', *Bulletin of the John Rylands Library* **32**, 1949-50, 229-300. Of Norbury Booths Hall. Lists 362 items, mainly relating to Cheshire.

Leicester

LEACH, JOAN. 'The Leicester of Tabley letters', *Cheshire history* 14, 1984, 21-2. Discussion of a collection of family letter and papers.

Mainwaring

FAWTIER, ROBERT. *Hand-list of the Mainwaring and Jodrell manuscripts at present in the custody of the John Rylands Library.* Manchester: the University Press, 1923. Reprinted with additions from *Bulletin of the John Rylands Library* 7, 1922-3, 143-67 & 279-89. Lists deeds and charters from numerous Cheshire parishes, also letters, genealogical rolls, papers, *etc.*

TOMKINS, H. BARR. 'Sir Philip Tatton Mainwaring, Bart., of Peover Hall, Cheshire', in HISTORICAL MANUSCRIPTS COMMISSION. *Tenth report, appendix, part IV.* H.M.S.O., 1885, 199-210. Includes summary description of estate papers, *etc.*

Malbane

WROTTESLEY, GEORGE. 'Charters of William Malbane', *Genealogist* N.S., 7, 1890, 192. 11th c.

Shakerley

STEWART-BROWN, R. 'Some Cheshire deeds', *C.Sf.* 3rd series 17, 1922, 107-8, 109, 109, & 113-5. Medieval deeds from the Shakerley collection.

Stanley

See Hoton

Talbot

BARKER, ERIC E., ed. *Talbot deeds 1200-1682.* L.C.R.S., 103. 1953. Includes folded pedigree of Domville of Brimstage and Oxton, and notes on Dunfont of Chester; medieval.

I[RVINE], W.F. 'The Shrewsbury (Talbot manuscripts)', *C.Sf.* 3rd series 33, 1939; 34, 1941, *passim.* Medieval deed abstracts.

Stanley

'The rental of Sir Rowland Stanley of Hooton, Kt., 24 Aug, 1592', *C.Sf.* 3rd series 52, 1957, 37-42, *passim.*

Thornton

'An early rental of Sir Peter de Thornton of Thornton-in-the-Moors, dated 1354', *C.Sf.* 3rd series 53-4, 55-66, 58-9, 60-61, 62-3.

Wilbraham

ROWE, F.G.C. 'Wilbraham of Nantwich', *C.Sf.* 3rd series 57, 1964, 34-40, *passim.* Deed abstracts, 16-17th c.

E. *Manorial descents.*

Many historians have worked out the descents of manors and other properties. The major work on this topic for Cheshire is:

FARRER, WILLIAM. *Honours and knights fees: an attempt to identify the component parts of certain honours and to trace the descent of the tenants of the same who held by Knight's service or serjeanty from the eleventh to the fourteenth century, volume II: Chester; Huntingdon.* Spottiswoode, Ballantyne & Co., 1924.

Bramhall Hall

DEAN, E.BARBARA. *Bramhall Hall: the story of an Elizabethan manor house.* Stockport: Stockport Metropolitan Borough Recreation & Culture Division, 1977. Traces descent, 11-20th c.

Chorley Hall

NORBURY, WILLIAM. 'Chorley Hall and other buildings in its neighbourhood, *L.C.A.S.* **4**, 1886, 99-114. Includes notes on descent; in Wilmslow township.

Gawsworth

RICHARDS, RAYMOND. *The manor of Gawsworth, Cheshire.* Ancient Monuments Society, 1957. Also published as *Transactions of the . . . Society* N.S., **5**, 1957, 1-356. Descent; includes pedigree of Orreby, Fitton and Gerrard, 13-18th c., also monumental inscriptions, lists of rectors, parish clerks, churchwardens, and schoolmasters, and extracts from a wide range of parish records.

Halton

BEAMONT, WILLIAM. *A history of the Castle of Halton and the Priory or Abbey of Norton, with an account of the Barons of Halton, the Priors and Abbots of Norton, and an account of Rock Savage and Daresbury church, with notices of the historic events of the neighbourhood.* Warrington: Percival Pearce, 1873. Descent.

Leasowe Castle

WOODS, E. CUTHBERT. 'Leasowe Castle: its owners and history', *H.S.L.C.* **73**; N.S., **37**, 127-48. Descent; also lists tenants of oxgangs at Wallasey, and Liscard, 1768.

Little Moreton Hall

HEAD, ROBERT. *Moreton Old Hall, with an account of its past and present owners.* Congleton: The Chronicle, 1914.

Newton Heath

FITCH, IAN C. 'The Windsor Road connection', *N.C.F.H.* **13**(3), 1986, 87-9; **13**(4), 1986, 107-8. Traces descent of houses, 19-20th c., in a Newton Heath street.

Poynton Park

SHERCLIFF, W.H. *Poynton Park: its lords and their mansions: Sir George Warren, the Bulkeley and Vernon families, and their contrbution to Poynton history.* Stockport: the author, 1988. Includes pedigree, 18-20th c.

Prestbury

RENAUD, FRANK, ed. *Contributions towards a history of the ancient parish of Prestbury in Cheshire.* Cm.S., O.S., **97**. 1876. Includes descents of various properties, with pedigrees (some folded) of Pigot, Legh, Danyers, *etc.*

RENAUD, FRANK. 'Early history of Prestbury parish church and manor, Cheshire', *L.C.A.S.* **13**, 1895, 1-18. Descent, to 16th c.

Wirral Hundred

STEWART-BROWN, RONALD. *The Wapentake of Wirral: a history of the royal franshise of the Hundred and Hundred court of Wirral in Cheshire, with an appendix containing a list of the officers and lords of the Hundred from the fourteenth century, a series of leases of the Hundred from 1352 to 1786, and the Crown grant of the Lordship of the Hundred in 1820.* Liverpool: Henry Young & Sons, 1907

11. RECORDS OF NATIONAL, COUNTY AND LOCAL ADMINISTRATION

A. *National and County*

The archives of national and county government are essential sources of information for the genealogist and many are referred to in other sections of this bibliography; for example, official lists of names are identified in section 8. Here are listed a wide range of works dealing with topics such as knights' fees, enclosure, accounts, legal suits, *etc.* These are listed chronologically, and are followed by a number of items dealing with the general records of the Palatinate and Quarter Sessions, and with lists of M.P.'s, J.P.'s, *etc.*

STEWART-BROWN, R., ed. *Cheshire in the pipe rolls, 1158-1301,* transcribed by Mabel H. Mills. L.C.R.S. 92. 1938.

STEWART-BROWN, R. 'Cheshire petitions', *C.Sf.* 3rd series 11, 1915, 9-10. Index of medieval petitions in the Public Record Office.

STEWART-BROWN, R. 'Cheshire in the Close and Patent rolls, 1237-1247', *C.Sf.* 3rd series 166, 1921, *passim.* Brief Cheshire extracts.

'Knights fees in Cheshire in 1252', *C.Sf.* 3rd series 5, 1904, 1. List from the *Red book of the Exchequer.*

STEWART-BROWN, R., ed. *Calendar of county court, city court, and eyre rolls of Chester 1259-1297, with an inquest of military service, 1288.* Cm.S., N.S., 84. 1925.

'Chester escheators' accounts, 1283-1354', *C.Sf.* 3rd series 26, 1934, 53-69, *passim.* Includes names of many Cheshire crown tenants.

'The Knights fees in 1300', *C.Sf.* 3rd series 5 1904, 15-16. See also 43.

LUMBY, J.H. 'Chester and Liverpool in the *patent rolls* of Richard II and the Lancastrian and Yorkist Kings', *H.S.L.C.* 55-6; N.S., 19-20, 1903-4, 1663-87. Includes list of men granted letters of protection to accompany Sir John Stanley in Ireland, 1386-91.

BOOTH, P.H.W., & CARR, A.D., eds. *Account of Master John de Burnham the younger, Chamberlain of Chester, of the revenues of the Counties of Chester and Flint, Michaelmas 1361 to Michaelmas 1362.*

L.C.R.S., 125. 1991. Includes extensive biographical notes on personages mentioned.

'Lancastrian rising at Nantwich', *C.Sf.* 3rd series 22, 1927, 14-15. Includes list of jurors and rebels, 1471.

STEWART-BROWN, R. 'Cheshire men in 1509-10, etc', *C.Sf.* 3rd series 18, 1923, 55-6. List of pardons from the *pardon rolls.*

LEADAM, I.S., ed. *The domesday of inclosures, 1517-1518, being the extant returns to Chancery for Berkshire, Buckinghamshire, Cheshire, Essex, Leicestershire, Lincolnshire, Northamptonshire, Oxfordshire and Warwickshire, by the Commissioners of Inclosures in 1517, and for Bedfordshire in 1518, together with Dugdale's ms. notes of the Warwickshire inquisitions in 1517, 1518 and 1549.* 2 vols. Longmans, Green & Co., 1897. Names many landlords.

STEWART-BROWN, R., ed. *Lancashire and Cheshire cases in the Court of Star Chamber.* L.C.R.S. 71. 1916. Pt.1. No more published. Abstracts of 108 suits, early 16th c.

This is supplemented by:

B[ENNETT], J.H.E. 'Calendar of Star Chamber proceedings *C.Sf.* 3rd series 20, 1924, 87-8.

See also:

'Star Chamber cases from Cheshire', *C.Sf.* 3rd series 5, 1904, *passim.* List, 16th c.

FISHWICK, CAROLINE, ed. *A calendar of Lancashire and Cheshire Exchequer depositions by commission, from 1558 to 1702.* L.C.R.S. 11. 1885.

C., E.R. 'Some Cheshire suits', *C.Sf.* 3rd series 20, 1924, 39, 43-4 & 48. Lists deponents, 1562-70.

HALL, JAMES. 'The feodary returns for Cheshire in the 18th Elizabeth, 1576', *J.C.A.H.S.* N.S., 17, 1910, 19-54. Discussion of a return of payments made from Cheshire estates to the Court of Wards; includes many extracts with names.

EARWAKER, J.P., ed. 'Obligatory Knighthood, *temp.* Charles I: lists of the esquires and gentlemen in Cheshire and Lancashire who refused the order of Knighthood at the coronation of Charles I, drawn up in the years 1631 and 1632', in *Miscellanies relating to Lancashire and Cheshire.* 1. L.C.R.S. 12. 1885, 191-223.

'Cheshire records transcribed from the originals in the Public Record Office', *J.C.A.H.S.* N.S. 6(3), 1899, 283-345. From the Royalist Composition Papers, covering royalists who were fined for their 'malignity' during the Civil War.

'Sequestrators' accounts for Wirral, 1644-1648', *C.Sf.* 3rd series 50, 1958, 27-43. Accounts *etc.,* of the Parliamentary administration of Royalist estates.

RODWAY, ALFRED, J. 'The order of the Royal Oak', *C.N.Q.* 7, 1887, 144. List of those to be nominated in Lancashire and Cheshire, 1660.

HALL, JAMES. 'Cheshire gentry in 1745', *C.Sf.* 3rd series 5, 1904, 105-66. List of subscribers to a fund for 'regulating and reducing the expenses attending the office of sheriff'.

'County of Chester', in *Abstracts of the returns of charitable donations for the benefit of poor persons, made by the minister and churchwardens of the several parishes and townships in England and Wales 1786-1788.* House of Commons Parliamentary papers, 1816, XVIA, 121-72. Summary list of benefactors.

Palatinate of Chester.

The existence of the Palatinate meant that the government of Cheshire was not constituted in the same way as in other counties; the Palatinate had courts which replicated some of those in London. For general accounts of the medieval Palatinate, see:

ALEXANDER, JAMES W. 'New evidence on the Palatinate of Chester', *English historical review* 85, 1970, 715-29.

BARRACLOUGH, GEOFFREY. 'The Earldom and County Palatine of Chester', *H.S.L.C.* 103, 1951, 23-57.

THACKER, A.T. *The Earldom of Chester and its charters: a tribute to Geoffrey Barraclough.* Chester: Chester Archaeological Society, 1991. Published as *J.C.A.H.S.* 71. 1991.

STEWART-BROWN, R. 'The end of the Norman Earldom of Chester', *English historical review* 35, 1920, 2-54.

BOOTH, P.H.W. *The financial administration of the lordship and county of Chester, 1272-1377.* Cm.S., 3rd series 28. 1981. General study.

CLAYTON, DOROTHY J. *The administration of the County Palatine of Chester, 1442-1485.* CmS., 3rd series 35. 1990. Includes bibliography.

A brief description of Palatine records for genealogists is given in:

JACKSON, M.N. 'Further Cheshire sources in the Public Record Office', *N.C.F.H.* 6(4), 1979, 110-11.

Much older and now outdated descriptions are given in the following articles. The records are now at the Public Record Office, and not, as these articles state, at Chester Castle.

BLACK, W.H. 'On the records of the County Palatine of Chester' *Journal of the British Archaeological Association* 5, 1850, 187-95.

BLACK, W.H. 'On the records at Chester Castle', *J.C.A.H.S.* 1(3), 1852, 312-26. Lecture on Palatinate records.

For the functions of the various Palatinate courts, see:

TALLENT-BATEMAN, CHAS. T. 'The ancient Lancashire and Cheshire courts of civil jurisdiction', *L.C.A.S.* 4, 1886, 61-79. Lists the various courts, whose records may have genealogical value.

TALLENT-BATEMAN, CHAS.T. 'The ancient Lancashire and Cheshire courts of criminal and special jurisdiction', *L.C.A.S.* 5, 1887, 231-41.

For a full calendar of Palatine records, see:

'Palatinate of Chester', in *List of records of the Palatinates of Chester, Durham and Lancaster, the Honour of Peveril and the Principality of Wales, preserved in the Public Record Office.* Lists and indexes, 40. Amended ed. New York: Kraus Reprint, 1963, 1-29.

See also:

BLACK, WILLIAM HENRY. 'Report . . . on a survey and examination of the records of the Court of Session and Exchequer of the County Palatine of Chester, and the Court of Great Sessions of the Principality of Wales . . .', *First report of the Deputy Keeper of the Public Records.* H.M.S.O., 1840, 78-122. Includes summary listing.

The early charters of the Earldom of Chester are printed in:

BARRACLOUGH, GEOFFREY, ed. *The charters of the Anglo-Norman Earls of Chester, c. 1071-1237.* L.C.R.S., 126. 1988.

See also:

BARRACLOUGH, GEOFFREY, ed. 'Some charters of the Earl of Chester', in BARNES, PATRICIA M., & SLADE, C.F., eds. *A medieval miscellany for Doris Mary Stenton.* Pipe Roll Society publication, 74; N.S., 36, 1962, 25-43.

More detailed editions of records *etc.* include:

STEWART-BROWN, RONALD, ed. *Accounts of the chamberlains and other officers of the County of Chester, 1301-1360* . . . L.C.R.S. 59. 1910.

Register of Edward the Black Prince preserved in the Public Record Office. Part 3 (Palatinate of Chester), A.D. 1351-1365. H.M.S.O., 1932.

BOOTH, P.H.W. 'Calendar of the Cheshire *trailbaston* proceedings, 1353', *Cheshire history* 11, 1983, 39-51; 12, 1983, 24-8; 13, 1984, 22-8; 14, 1985, 23-6; 16, 1985, 21-5.

HARRIS, B.E., & CLAYTON, DOROTHY J. 'Criminal procedure in Cheshire in the mid fifteenth century', *H.S.L.C.* 128, 1979, 161-72. Includes discussion of the records of the Palatinate's county court.

CLAYTON, DOROTHY J. 'Peace bonds and the maintainance of law and order in late medieval England: the example of Cheshire', *Bulletin of the Institute of Historical Research* 58, 1985, 133-48. General study of a little used source.

'Welsh records: Calendar of recognizance rolls of the Palatinate of Chester, from the beginning of the reign of Henry V to the end of the reign of Henry VII', *Thirty-seventh annual report of the Deputy Keeper of the Public Records* 1876, pt. 2 appendix 2, 1-819; *Thirtyninth* . . ., 1878, appendix, 1-306.

RHODES, E.H. 'Welsh records: calendar of bills and answers, &c., Henry 8, Edward 6, and Philip and Mary', *Twenty-fifth annual report of the Deputy Keeper of the Public Records.* H.M.S.O., 1864, 23-31. Actually proceedings in the Exchequer Court of Chester. Supplemented by:

B., J. 'Chester Exchequer bills', *C.Sf.* 3rd series, 21, 1926, 17-18, 19-20, & 21-2, & 23.

TALLENT-BATEMAN, CHAS. 'Notes on the ancient Court of Exchequer at Chester', *L.C.A.S.* 14, 1896, 139-48. Describes procedure.

RHODES, E.H. 'Calendar of all warrants, signed bills, and privy seals, of the reigns of Hen. VII and Hen. VIII, with one of Hen. VI and one of Elizabeth, removed from Chester to the Public Record Office in 1854', *Twenty sixth annual report of the Deputy Keeper of the Public Records* 1865, 16-31. For Cheshire and Flintshire.

RHODES, E.H. 'Welsh records: calendar of all writs of general livery, ouster-le-main, &c., Elizabeth, James I and Charles I . . .', *Twenty-sixth annual report of the Deputy Keeper of the Public Records* 1865, 32-5. In the Palatinate of Cheshire.

Quarter Sessions.

For a general introduction to Quarter Sessions records, see:

DEWHURST, J.C. 'The Quarter Sessions records of the County Palatine of Chester', *J.C.A.H.S.* N.S., 32(1), 1937, 53-63.

A full calendar is provided by:

BENNETT, J.H.E., & DEWHURST, J.C. *Quarter sessions records, with other records of the justices of the peace for the County Palatine of Chester, 1559-1760, together with a few earlier miscellaneous records deposited with Cheshire County Council.* L.C.R.S. 94. 1940. v.1. No more published.

An important microfilm edition of the original records is also available:

Justice and authority in England: County Quarter Sessions and related records. Series 1: Cheshire. 53 microfilm reels. Brighton: Harvester Microfilm, 1985. Contents: Pt.1. Recognizances and orders, 1559-1650. Indictments and presentments, 1557-1662. Recognizances, orders, indictments and presentments, 1660-1818. Pt.2. Quarter Sessions files, 1571 (Michaelmas)-1603 (Easter) Pt.3. Quarter Sessions files, 1603 (Trinity)-1616 (Michaelmas).

Other useful works include:

MORRILL, J.S. *The Cheshire Grand Jury 1625-1659: a social and administrative study.* Leicester University Dept. of English Local History, occasional papers, 3rd series 1. Leicester: Leicester University Press, 1976. Includes list of the most active grand jurors.

S., A.G. 'Bails granted at the Sessions of Chester, 1663-4 and 1679-80', *C.Sf.* 3rd series 14, 1919, 12-34, *passim.* Calendar.

Lists of officers, etc.

An extensive general listing of Palatinate officers is given in:

TURNER, PETER. 'List of officers of the Palatinate of Chester, in the Counties of Chester and Flint, and North Wales, from the earliest period to the extinction of the Welsh judicature', *Thirty-first annual report of the Deputy Keeper of the Public Records* 1870, appendix, 169-261.

For sheriffs, see:

HISTORICUS. 'Cheshire high sheriffs', *C.N.Q.* **6**, 1886, 133-7 & 215-7. See also N.S., **1**, 1896, 1-6.

'Sheriffs of Cheshire', *Cheshire & Lancashire historical collector* **6**, 1853, 80. List, 1818-50.

Members of Parliament are listed in:

PINK, W. DUNCOMBE, & BEAVEN, A.B. 'Parliamentary representation of Cheshire', *L.G.* **1**, 1879-80, 371-81, 405-20 & 458-71. 16-19th c.

M., R. 'Parliamentary representation of Chester, city and county', *C.Sf.* **2-3**, 1883-91, *passim.*

There are various lists of Justices of the Peace:

'Commission of the Peace for Cheshire in 1554', *C.Sf.* 3rd series **17**, 1922, 86-7.

'Justices of the Peace for Cheshire, 1601', *C.Sf.* 3rd series **1**, 1896, 11.

'The names of the Justices of the Peace in Cheshire in 1603', *C.Sf.* N.S., **1**, 1895, 146-8.

'Justices of the Peace in Cheshire in 1620', *C.Sf.* 3rd issue **1**, 1896, 23.

'New magistrates for Cheshire in 1758', *C.Sf.* N.S., **1** 1895, 99-100.

B. *Local*

The records of parochial and township government - churchwardens' accounts, rate lists, poor law records, *etc.* - contain a great deal of information valuable to the genealogist. They frequently provide the names of the humble mass of the poor who otherwise went unrecorded. Those which have been published are listed here.

Adlington

'Adlington Association', *N.C.F.H.* **14**(4), 1987, 125. Lists members of an association for protection against crime, 1811.

Altrincham

'Persons qualified to serve on juries in the Township of Altrincham, October 1st, 1798', *N.C.F.H.* **15**(1), 1988, 22. List.

Barrow

SYNGE, K. 'Index of names on the tithe map schedule for Barrow, Cheshire, 1845', *F.H.S.C.J.* **3**(2), 1972, 14.

Bunbury

E., J.C. 'Bunbury parish books', *C.Sf.* **2**, 1883, 187-8 & 192-3. 17-19th c. extracts.

Burland

W., J. 'Some Burland notes', *C.Sf.* 3rd series **5**, 1904, 110. Extracts from an overseer's notebook, 1831-5.

Cheadle Bulkeley

B., W.H. 'Cheadle Bulkeley in 1731', *A.N.Q.* **2**, 1883, 5-6. Poor rate levy.

UNSWORTH, CATH. 'Poor rate assessments for Cheadle Bulkeley, 1731', *N.C.F.H.* **14**(3), 1987, 90-91.

Chester

Many Chester records have been printed. For a general introduction see:

GROOMBRIDGE, MARGARET J. 'Introduction to the records of the city of Chester', *Cheshire historian* **2**, 1952, 34-40.

Two important calendars of city records are available:

GROOMBRIDGE, MARGARET J. *Guide to the charters, plate and insigna of the city of Chester.* [Chester: City Council, 1950.]

JEAFFRESON, J.C. 'Manuscripts of the Corporation of the City of Chester', in HISTORICAL MANUSCRIPTS COMMISSION. *Eighth report . . .* H.M.S.O., 1881, pt.1, 355-403.

See also:

'Chester City records', *C.Sf.* 3rd series **55**, 1960, *passim.* List of recent acquisitions.

CLOPPER, LAWRENCE M., ed. *Chester.* Records of early English drama. Toronto: University of Toronto Press; Manchester University Press, 1979. Numerous extracts from city records.

I[RVINE] W.F. 'The annals of Chester', *C.Sf.* 3rd series **29-30**, 1935-6, *passim.* Includes much information on civic matters.

Various lists of officers are available:

I[RVINE], W.F. 'A new list of the mayors and sheriffs of the City of Chester from the year 1238', *C.Sf.* 3rd series **34**, 1941, *passim.*

'A list of the mayors of Chester', *C.Sf.* 3rd series **28**, 1935, 41-2. 1481-1715; from St. Michael's parish.

FOREMAN, JOHN GRINDLEY. 'Borough and City of Chester grand jury list: April 8th, 1853', *F.H.S.C.J.* **10**(3), 1981, 10.

M. Officers of the Corporation of Chester, 1703 to 1704', *C.Sf.* 3rd series, **13**, 1918, 83. List.

Freemen are listed in :

BENNETT, J.H.E., ed. *The rolls of the freemen of the City of Chester.* L.C.R.S. **51** & **55**. 1906-8. Pt.1. 1392-1700. Pt.2. 1700-1805.

For the city guilds, see:

GROOMBRIDGE, MARGARET J. 'The city guilds of Chester', *J.C.A.H.S.* **39**, 1952, 93-108. Survey of archives: admissions registers, minutes, accounts *etc.*

FEARNALL, H. 'Freemen and Guilds of the City of Chester', *F.H.S.C.J.* **3**(3) 1972, 11-13. Brief note on guild records, including list of freemen admitted to the Butchers' Guild, 1806-1946.

A variety of other works are available; they are listed here in rough chronological order:

HOPKINS, A., ed. *Selected rolls of the Chester city courts; late thirteenth and early fourteenth centuries.* Cm.S., 3rd series **2**. 1950.

'The bounds of the City of Chester', *C.Sf.* **2** 1883, 30-32. Lists citizens who beat the bounds, 1573.

GROOMBRIDGE, MARGARET J., ed. *Calendar of Chester city council minutes, 1603-1642.* L.C.R.S., **106**. 1956.

MORRIS, RUPERT H. 'Side lights on the Civil War in Cheshire, 1643-5', *J.C.A.H.S.* N.S., **6**(3), 1899, 346-94. Includes list of householders in Chester during the siege, 1645.

B[ENNETT], J.H.E. 'Some orders of assembly regarding Chester freemen', *C.Sf.* 3rd series **20**, 1924, 92. Notes on freemen admissions, early 18th c.

BOULTON, H.E. 'The Chester Infirmary', *J.C.A.H.S.* **47**, 1960, 9-19. Includes list of records.

RIDEOUT, EDNA. 'The account book of the New Haven, Chester', *H.S.L.C.* **80**, 1928, 86-128. Transcript, giving many names of workmen.

RIDEOUT, EDNA. 'The Chester companies and the Old Quay', *H.S.L.C.* **79**, 1927, 141-74. Includes transcript of a levy made on tradesmen for the maintainance of the quay, 1559.

BENNETT, J.H.E. 'Valentine Broughton's Charity', *C.Sf.* 3rd series **8**, 1911, *passim.* In Chester; includes lists of recipients, 17th c.

C., M. 'Chester treasurers' accounts, 1612-1619', *C.Sf.* 4th series **6**, 1969, 28-45. Many names.

B[ENNETT], J.H.E. 'Support of the foreign policy of William III by Chester citizens', *C.Sf.* 3rd series **14**, 1919, 7-8. Lists citizens who took an oath.

'Some Chester orders of Assembly', *C.Sf.* 3rd series **27**, 1927, 28-9 & 30-3. Notes from the Assembly book, 1707-10.

'Extracts from Chester city gaol and house of correction records', *N.C.F.H.* **15**(3), 1988, 90-91. Names some inmates, 1808-30.

B[URNE], R.V.H. 'Eastgate in 1750', *C.Sf.* 3rd series **56**, 1963, 89-92, *passim.* Lists inhabitants at Eastgate, Chester.

Holy Trinity

BERESFORD, J.R. 'The churchwardens' accounts of Holy Trinity, Chester, 1532 to 1633', *J.C.A.H.S.* **38**, 1951, 95-172. Full transcript; with many names; for index, see 191-202. (This indexes the whole journal)

St. Bridget

BARBER, E. 'The churchwardens' accounts of the parish of S. Bridget, Chester, 1811-1847', *J.C.A.H.S.* N.S., **11**, 1904, 524. General discussion.

St. John

SCOTT, S. COOPER. 'Extracts from the churchwardens' accounts and vestry minutes of St. John's, Chester', *J.C.A.H.S.* N.S., **3**, 1890, 48-70.

St. Martin

BARBER, E. 'The churchwardens' accounts of S. Martin's, Chester, from 1683 to 1816', *J.C.A.H.S.* N.S., **12**, 1905, 22-38. General discussion.

St. Mary on the Hill

EARWAKER, J.P. 'The ancient parish books of the church of St. Mary-on-the-Hill, Chester', *J.C.A.H.S.* N.S., **2**, 1888, 132-48.

WHITTELL, H.M. *'Index nominum* to the churchwardens' accounts of St. Marys on the Hill, Chester, 1536 to 1565', *C.Sf.* 3rd series **29**, 1935, 55-97, *passim.* Index to the accounts printed in Earwaker & Morris's *History of the church . . .* (see section 5 above)

'Churchwardens' accounts of St. Mary's on the Hill, Chester, 1574-5', *C.Sf.* 3rd series 13, 1918, 58, 60 & 61-2.

WILSON, MRS. 'Chester St. Mary's settlement papers', *F.H.S.C.J.* 5(2), 1976, 13; 5(3), 1976, 11-12. List.

St. Michael

EARWAKER, J.P. 'Notes on the registers and churchwardens' accounts of St. Michael, Chester', *J.C.A.H.S.* N.S., 3, 1890, 26-44.

Church Hulme

'Parish of Church Hulme: settlement certificates', *F.H.S.C.J.* 6(1), 1976, 12-13; 6(2), 1977, 6.

PLANT, W.K. 'Church Hulme settlement certificates and removal orders', *F.H.S.C.J.* 13(2), 1983. 3-4. List, mid-18th c.

Church Lawton

F., A.J. 'Church Lawton constables' accounts, 1642-1646', *C.Sf.* 3rd series 57, 1964, 41-4, *passim.*

NUNN, H. 'A list of the constables who served in Lawton court leet from 1634 to 1766', *A.N.Q.* 4, 1884, 65-6 & 118-9. See also 5, 1885, 26-7 for continuation *etc.,* to 1863.

Coddington

T., W.F.J. 'Some Coddington benefactors', *C.Sf.* 3rd series 20 1924, 102-3. See also 104-5.

Congleton

'Congleton accounts', *C.N.Q.* N.S. 5, 1900. 6-8. Borough accounts, 16-17th c.

Crewe

HALL, JAMES. 'Constables accounts for Crewe', *C.Sf.* 2, 1883, 220-21 & 224-6. 17-18th c.

Cuddington

'Cuddington (near Northwich) tithe account, 1839', *F.H.S.C.J.* 4(1), 1973, 10. Brief list of owners and occupiers.

TIMMIS, G.H. 'Cuddington (nr. Northwich) inclosure account, 1766', *F.H.S.C.J.* 3(4), 1972, 9. List of land owners and tenants.

Davenham

R., F.G.C. 'Davenham parish terrier, 1696', *C.Sf.* 3rd series 55, 1960, 15-16.

Dodleston

F., A.J. 'Records of St. Mary's parish church, Dodleston', *C.Sf.* 3rd series 56, 1963, 61-5, *passim.* Brief list with some extracts.

Frodsham

'Frodsham churchwardens' books', *C.Sf.* 3rd series 1, 1896, 97, 109-10 & 119. Includes extract from accounts, 1633, with many names.

Fulshaw

See Pownall Fee

Goostrey

'Goostrey churchwardens' accounts', *C.Sf.* 3rd series 56, 1963, 87. See also 93 & 99-100; 57, 1964, 1-2. Extracts, 1648.

Grappenhall

HODGKINSON, ARTHUR. 'The accounts of the surveyors of the highways for the township of Grappenhall, 1732-1829', *L.C.A.S.* 48, 1932, 95-116. General discussion, with many extracts.

R[YLANDS,] J.P. 'The mize of Grappenhall and Latchford', 1748', *C.Sf.* 3rd series 13, 1918, 47-8. Lists taxpayers.

Geat Boughton

TUSHINGHAM, T.P. 'Assessment of Great Boughton in 1708', *C.Sf.* 3rd series 10, 1914, 23, 25 & 33.

T[USHINGHAM], T.P. 'Assessment of Great Boughton in 1753', *C.Sf.* 3rd series 10, 1914, 117 & 121.

Great Budworth

BOYD, A.W. 'The Great Budworth churchwardens' accounts in the eighteenth century', *L.C.A.S.* 49, 1933, 12-74.

Great Warford

DALE, ALAN. 'John Norbury's three manuscript books', *Lancashire and Cheshire historian* 1-2, 1965-66, *passim.* Abstracts of various parish records from Great Warford.

Handley

BENNETT, J.H.E. 'Handley parish records', *C.Sf.* 3rd series **5**, 1904, 87-8. Assessment for trained soldiers, 1711.

Heaton Norris

VAUGHAN, J. LINGARD. 'Ancient Heaton Norris poor rate', *A.N.Q.* **2**, 1883, 187. Assessment, 1724.

Latchford

See Grappenhall

Macclesfield

'Macclesfield collection', *Lancashire and Cheshire historian* **2**, 1966, 391-6, 421-4 & 451-6; **3**, 1967, 593-6. Calendar of borough archives.

CLARKE, W.H. 'On the charters, documents and insignia relating to the ancient manor and borough of Macclesfield', *L.C.A.S.* **22**, 1904, 154-69.

Macclesfield Forest

'Settlement certificates, Macclesfield Forest', *N.C.F.H.* **18**(1), 1991, 9. List, 1698-1729.

Malpas

KENYON, W.T. 'Malpas town, parish and church', *J.C.A.H.S.* N.S., **3**, 1890, 162-74. Includes list of parish records.

Middlewich

O'RIORDAN, CHRISTOPHER. 'Civil war squatters in the Middlewich House of Correction', *Cheshire history* **18**, 1986, 21-3.

VAUDREY, B.LL. 'Some notes on the parish church of Middlewich, Cheshire', *H.S.L.C.* **27**; 3rd series **3**, 1875, 1-12. Extracts from churchwardens' accounts, 1635 & 1715.

Mobberley

'The old spinning wheel', *C.N.Q.* N.S., **8**, 1908-11, 143-5. Includes extracts from Mobberley overseers accounts, late 18th c., many names.

Nantwich

CHURCH, CONNIE. 'The affray in Wood Street, Nantwich, 1572', *F.H.S.C.J.* **7**(4), 1978, 16-17. Includes extensive list of witnesses; also 'list of gentlemen and freeholders resident in Nantwich, 1579'.

Neston

CHEETHAM, F.H. 'The bells of the parish church of Neston, Cheshire', *L.C.A.S.* **48**, 1932, 166-29. Includes many extracts from churchwardens' accounts, 18-19th c.

Newton by Daresbury

See Sevenoaks

Northen Etchells

CRAMPTON, JOHN, CLARKE, JOHN & OCCLESTONE, THOS. *Survey and valuation of the township of Northen and Stockport Etchells.* Manchester: J. Gleave, 1821.
See also Northenden

Northenden

'[Tithe apportionments]', *C.F.H.* **5**, 1975, 18-19. Lists landowners and occupiers of Northenden, 1841, Northen Etchells, 1841, and Stockport Etchells, 1839; also Didsbury, Lancashire, 1845.

Overchurch

JONES, W.G.H. 'Overchurch parish church and the township of Upton', *H.S.L.C.* **111**, 1959, 77-92. Includes list of parish records, assessments of 1731 and 1752, and list of vicars, 16-20th c.

Pownall Fee

NORBURY, WILLIAM. 'Pownall Fee old parish chest', *L.C.A.S.* **3**, 1885, 39-44. Brief description of contents.

NORBURY, WILLIAM. 'Township of Pownall Fee and Fulshaw', *A.N.Q.* **4-9**, 1884-9, *passim.* Extracts from township records, mainly 18th c.

Poynton

DICKEN, JOAN. 'Local government records of the townships of Poynton and Worth', *Poynton Local History Society newsletter* **7**, 1983, 11-12. Includes brief list, 19-20th c.

Pulford

MAX, L.P. 'Tithe collected in the parish of Pulford in 1591', *C.Sf.* 3rd series **20**, 1924, 14-15. See also 22.

Sandbach

S[TEWART]-B[ROWN], R. 'Petition of the parishioners of Sandbach', *C.Sf.* 3rd series **9**, 1913, 61. Lists petitions, mid-17th c.

CHADWICK, PETER. 'An 1831 census for Sandbach?', *F.H.S.C.J.* **17**(1), 1987, 5. Lists various surveys made for administrative purposes, which provide lists of owners and occupiers.

'A Sandbach survey of 1858', *F.H.S.C.J.* **17**(2), 1987, 7-8. Lists landowners and occupiers.

Sevenoaks

BOYD, ARNOLD W. 'The town books of Sevenoaks, and Newton-by-Daresbury, Cheshire', *L.C.A.S.* **45**, 1928, 44-88.

Stoak

'Stoak churchwardens' accounts', *C.Sf.* 3rd series **37**, 1948, *passim.* 17-19th c..

Stockport

Stockport poor rate, 1731 and 1781: indexes of people and places. Handlist **5**. Stockport: Metropolitan Borough of Stockport Library of Local Studies, 1975.

List of burgesses within the manor of Stockport, 1835. Handlist **12**. Stockport: Metropolitan Borough of Stockport, Local Studies Library, 1979.

'Law and order in Stockport, 1853', *F.H.S.C.J.* **16**(4), 1987, 4-5. Reprinted from *C.N.Q.* Lists officers appointed by the Court Leet of the Borough.

Stockport Etchells

See Northenden

Upton

HANCE, E.M. 'Extracts from the parish records of Upton', *H.S.L.C.* **37**, N.S., **1**, 1885, 141-8. Includes 'assessment of a layard half for 1752', *etc.*

See also Overchurch

Wallasey

Acts of Parliament and provisional orders relating to Wallasey 1809-1899. Liverpool: C. Tinling & Co., 1899. Includes the Commissioners account for Wallasey enclosure, 1866, naming landowners.

West Kirby

'Bordland tithes in the parish of West Kirby', *C.Sf.* 3rd series **23**, 1928, 5-29, *passim.* Discussion of an Exchequer case of 1639; many names.

Wettenhall

RIDGWAY, MAURICE H. 'The Wettenhall parish book', *Cheshire historian* **6**, 1956, 34-41.

Whitegate

'Extracts from the church wardens accounts of Whitegate, Co. Chester, 1601 to 1662', *C.Sf.* N.S., **1**, 1895, 130-31 & 133-4.

Wirral

A., F.S. 'Early landowners in Wirral', *C.Sf.* 3rd series **17**, 1927, 101. Lists of jurors, 1259-60, from the Chester plea rolls.

THOMPSON, D.N. 'Wirral hospital records', *Journal of the Society of Archivists* **7**, 1985, 421-42. Discusses the problems of an archivist trying to locate, identify, and collect them.

IRVINE, W.F. 'Trespasses in the Forest of Wirral in 1351', *H.S.L.C.* **101**, 1949, 39-45. Transcript of a writ listing many names.

'Breakers of the forest law in Wirral', *C.Sf.* 3rd series **28**, 1935, 3-9. Includes schedule of offenders bound over, 1351.

Worth

See Poynton

12. ECCLESIASTICAL RECORDS.

A. *Church of England*

The role of the church in pre-industrial England was much wider than it is today. This fact is reflected in the wide range of ecclesiastical records available to the genealogist. Some of these - parish registers, probate records, churchwardens' accounts, *etc.,* - are dealt with in other sections of this book. This section focuses on those records which are more directly concerned with ecclesiastical administration. For general background on the church in Cheshire, consult:

MORRIS, RUPERT H. *Chester.* Diocesan histories. Society for Promoting Christian Knowledge, 1895.

MORANT, ROLAND, W. *Cheshire churches: a guide to the ancient parish churches of the county, 1066 to 1820.* Countywise, 1989. General study; little of genealogical interest.

RICHARDS, RAYMOND. *Old Cheshire churches: a survey of their history, fabric and furniture, with records of the older monuments.* B.T. Batsford, 1947. Includes lists of clergy, *etc.*

A variety of records, lists, and other works on diocesan administration have been published and are listed here in rough chronological order:

'Register of Bishop Stretton', *C.Sf.* 3rd series **55**, 1960, *passim.* 1360-84.

BENNETT, M.J. 'The Lancashire and Cheshire clergy, 1379', *H.S.L.C.* **124**, 1972, 1-30. Includes transcript of the clerical poll tax return for the Archdeaconry of Chester, 1379, listing clergy.

IRVINE, WM. FERGUSSON, ed. 'A list of the clergy in eleven deaneries of the Diocese of Chester, 1541-42, together with a list of the tenths and subsidy payable in ten deaneries [circa 1538]', in *Miscellanies relating to Lancashire and Cheshire* **3**. L.C.R.S. **33**. 1896. Separately paginated.

IRVINE, WM. FERGUSSON, ed. 'The earliest ordination book of the Diocese of Chester, 1542-7 and 1555-8', in *Miscellanies relating to Lancashire and Cheshire.* **4**. L.C.R.S. **43**. 1902. Separately paginated.

S., F. 'Cheshire clergy in 1559', *C.Sf.* 3rd series **3**, 1901, 11-12. See also *passim.* Lists clergy absent from visitation.

'Signatures to the three articles in Cheshire in 1563', *C.Sf.* 3rd series **1**, 1896, 33-5. Lists clergy who subscribed to an oath.

G., G.P. 'Religion in Cheshire in 1580', *C.Sf.* 3rd series **5**, 1904, 113-4. Lists gentry, noting religious stance.

IRVINE, WM. FERGUSSON. 'The Bishop of Chester's visitation book, 1592', *J.C.A.H.S.* N.S., 5(4), 1895, 384-426. Includes some extracts.

GRIGSON, FRANCIS. 'Institutions to Lancashire and Cheshire livings', *Lancashire and Cheshire antiquarian notes* **1**, 1885, 92-6, 111-6, 196-8, 203-5, 214-20 & 228-34; **2**, 1886, 24-6, 37-41, 67-79 & 113-26. Lists clergy, 17th c.

'Institutions to Cheshire livings', *A.N.Q.* **4**, 1884, 44-5 & 48-9. List, 17th c.

BRIDGEMAN, G.T.O., ed. 'Loans, contributions, subsidies and ship money paid by the clergy of the Diocese of Chester in the years 1620, 1622, 1624, 1635, 1636 and 1639 (as recorded in the private ledger of John Bridgeman, D.D., Bishop of Chester . . .)', in *Miscellanies relating to Lancashire and Cheshire* **1**. L.C.R.S., **12**, 1885, 43-129.

SHAW, W.A., ed. *Minutes of the Committee for the Relief of Plundered Ministers, and of the Trustees for the Maintainance of Ministers, relating to Lancashire and Cheshire, 1643-1660.* L.C.R.S. **28** & **34**. 1893-6. Pt.1. 1643-54. Pt.2. 1650-60.

AXON, ERNEST. 'Cheshire clergy in 1661', *C.Sf.* 3rd series **31**, 1937, 2-24, *passim.* Clergy contributions to the 'Free and voluntary present',

HUNTER, JOSEPH, ed. *Diary of Thomas Cartwright, Bishop of Chester, commencing at the time of his elevation to that see, August M.DC.LXXXVI, and terminating with the visitation of St. Mary Magdalene College, Oxford, October M.DC.LXXXVII.* Camden Society, O.S., **22**. 1843.

D[REDGE], J.I. 'The nonjurors of the Diocese of Chester', *P.N.* **2**, 1882, 238-40. Lists clergy refusing the oath of allegiance to William III.

BROWNBILL, JOHN, ed. 'List of clergymen &c., in the Diocese of Chester, 1691, recorded at the first visitation of Nicholas Stratford, Bishop of Chester', *Chetham miscellanies.* N.S., **3**. Cm.S., N.S., **73**. 1915. Separately paginated.

AXON, ERNEST. 'Cheshire clergy in 1696', *C.Sf.* 3rd series **31**, 1937, 28-35, *passim*. List from the Association oath roll.

The Chester Diocesan calendar, clergy list, and church almanack ... Chester: Hugh Roberts, 1857- . Title and publisher varies. Includes annual listing of clergy and other officers.

A number of publications provide information on the church in particular places. These are listed here.

Acton

'Acton church seating arrangements', *H.S.L.C.* **64**; N.S., **28**, 1912, 289-91. Lists 89 families.

Aston by Sutton

RICHARDS, RAYMOND. 'The lesser chapels of Cheshire: the church of St. Peter, Aston by Sutton', *H.S.L.C.* **102**, 1950, 115-35. Includes list of clergy, some inscriptions, *etc.*

Ashton upon Mersey

R., I.J.E. 'Seat-holders at Ashton-upon-Mersey parish church, 8 March, 1742', *P.N.* **3**, 1883, 235. List.

Barrow

W., H.M. 'The rectors of Barrow *C.Sf.* 3rd series **31**, 1937, 88-105; **32**, 1938, *passim*. See also **46**, 1952, 12. List, medieval.

Bidston

'The Rev. Richard Wright, curate of Bidston, 1667', *C.Sf.* 3rd series **1**, 1896, 35-7. Includes list of persons prepared to augment their minister's income.

Chester

JONES, DOUGLAS. *The church in Chester 1300-1540.* Cm.S., 3rd series **7**. 1956. Includes biographical notes on clergy, list of wills of citizens making bequests to city churches, *etc.*

BENNETT, J.H.E. 'The Black Friars of Chester', *J.C.A.H.S.* **39**, 1952, 29-58. Includes list of wardens, 13-16th c., list of tenants, 1544, *etc.*

EVANS, M.J.CROSSLEY. 'The clergy of the City of Chester, 1630-1672', *J.C.A.H.S.* **68**, 1985, 97-123. General study.

FORSHAW, F. 'Clerical Cestrians', *C.N.Q.* N.S., **5**, 1900, 91-4. Brief biographies of clergy.

St. Peter

SIMPSON, FRANK. *A history of the church of St. Peter in Chester, including quaint and interesting extracts from its old registers and a brief reference to its former surroundings.* Chester: G.R. Griffith, 1909, Includes extensive extracts from churchwardens' accounts, also biographical notes on rectors, list of churchwardens, *etc., etc.*

B[ENNETT], J.H.E. 'Two incumbents of St. Peters, Chester', *C.Sf.* 3rd series **13**, 1918, 13-15. Includes list of parishioners who petitioned for a new minister, c. 1663.

St. Werburgh

BURNE, R.V.H. *The monks of Chester: the history of St. Werburgh's Abbey.* S.P.C.K., 1962. Includes list of endowments, including names of benefactors, also rental of Ince, 1398, and a list of 'master craftsmen of the County Palatine, 1272-1550', by John Harvey.

'Abbey of St. Werburgh's, Chester: abbots, 1092-1540', *C.Sf.* 4th series **4**, 1969, 21-2. List.

TAYLOR, M.V., ed. 'Some obits of abbots and founders of St. Werburgh's Abbey, Chester, from a Bodleian ms', *L.C.R.S.* **64**, 1912, 81-111. Includes biographical notes.

'The chapter of St. Werburgh, Chester', *C.Sf.* 3rd series **46**, 1952, 49-52, *passim*. Lists of 1377 and 1538. For 1382 list, see **48**, 1956, 60.

BURNE, R.V.H. 'The dissolution of St. Werburgh's Abbey', *J.C.A.H.S.* **37**(1), 1948, 5-36. See also **37**(2), 1949, 312-3. Gives names of pensioned monks, annuitants, lessees, *etc.*

BURNE, R.V.H. *Chester Cathedral: from its founding by Henry VIII to the accession of Queen Victoria.* S.P.C.K., 1958. Includes lists of bishops and deans 16-20th c., also rental of Cathedral property, 1663.

HUGHES, T. 'Precentors of Chester Cathedral', *C.Sf.* **1**, 1879, 301. List, 1541-1877.

BURNE, R.V.H. 'Chester Cathedral, 1787-1837', *J.C.A.H.S.* **43**, 1956, 1-25. Includes biographical notes on clergy.

BURNE, R.V.H. 'Chester Cathedral in the eighteenth century', *J.C.A.H.S.* **41**, 1954, 39-61; **42**, 1955, 21-43. Includes biographical notes on clergy.

Christleton

G.-W., A.A. 'The pews of Christleton church in 1770', *C.Sf.* 3rd series **37**, 1948, 104-5 & 108-9. Lists pew holders.

Churton Heath

'A petition from the parishioners of Churton Heath chapel', *C.Sf.* 3rd series **1**, 1896, 29. Lists some 50 petitioners to the Committee for Plundered Ministers, 1646.

Eastham

CONNAH, G.E. 'Benefactors of Eastham parish', *C.Sf.* 3rd series **44**, 1950, 40-41. From a tablet in the church.

Farndon

'Subscribers to the repair of Farndon church, 1658', *C.Sf.* 3rd series **7**, 1910, 76 & 78. List.

Frodsham

'Frodsham church roll, 1495', *C.Sf.* 3rd series **4**, 1903, 79-81. List of seat holders.
'Frodsham church roll, 1637 & 1747', *C.Sf.* 3rd series **5**, 1904, 49-50, 66-7 & 70-71. Lists of seat owners.

Goostrey

YOUNG, PERCY M. 'A village choir in the age of reform', 1848-58', *Musical times* **128**, 1987, 225-9. Includes names of choristers at Goostrey.

Grappenhall

R[YLANDS,] J.P, ed. 'A terrier of the glebe lands belonging to the Rectory of Grappenhall', *C.Sf.* 3rd series **16**, 1921, 19. 1696.

Great Budworth

'[Seat roll for the church of Great Budworth, 1775]', *F.H.S.C.J.* **2**(2), 1971, 10-11; **2**(3) 1971, 66-9.

Haslington

'1709 brief: township of Haslington (parish of Barthomley)', *N.C.F.H.* **7**(4), 1980, 109. Lists contributors towards the relief and settlement of the 'poor distressed Palatines'.

Knutsford

BULLOCK, CONNIE. '1686 Knutsford inhabitants and its dissenters', *F.H.S.C.J.* **11**(1) 1981, 9-10.

Macclesfield

FINNEY, I.A. 'Benefactions to churches', *A.N.Q.* **2**, 1883, 210 & 213-4. Lists benefactions to St. Michaels, Macclesfield.

Mobberley

BOWLAND, JAS. 'Advowson of Mobberley', *A.N.Q.* **5**, 1885, 95. Lists clergy, 1281-1832.

Neston

I[RVINE], W.F. 'Vicars of Neston in the 16th century', *C.Sf.* 3rd series **50**, 1958, 46-52. And 17th c.
'A dispute relating to pews in Neston church, in 1711', *C.Sf.* 3rd series **2**, 1898, 51-2. See also 125. Lists inhabitants who petitioned the Bishop, 1711.
LEOPARD. 'Gallery in Neston church', *C.Sf.* 3rd series **7**, 1910, 61. Lists those who opposed its construction, early 18th c.

Poynton

SHERCLIFF, W.H. 'Lady Bulkeley's Charity, 1828 to present day', *Poynton Local History Society newsletter* **7**, 1983, 13-20. Gives some names of recipients in Poynton.
SHERCLIFF, W.H. 'The terrier of the pews in Poynton chapel in 1741', *Poynton Local History Society newsletter* **11**, 1985, 23-4. Lists pew renters.

Sandbach

SIMPSON, EILEEN. 'Sandbach citizens, witnesses to church enlargement, 1596', *F.H.S.C.J.* **16**(1), 1986, 10-12.
'Rectors of Sandbach', *C.N.Q.* **6**, 1886, 130. List, 14-20th c.

Shocklach

B[ENNETT], J.H.E. 'Incumbents of Shocklach', *C.Sf.* 3rd series **16**, 1921, 72. List, 1541-1901.

Stoak

B[ENNETT], J.H.E. 'The incumbents of Stoak', *C.Sf.* 3rd series **40**, 1948, *passim*. List with biographical notes, medieval-20th c.

Stockport

'The rectors of Stockport', *C.N.Q.* N.S., **6**, 1901, 63-8. Includes list.

Thornton Le Moors

B[ENNETT], J.H.E. 'The clergy of Thornton-in-the-Moors *C.Sf.* 3rd series **37**, 1948, *passim*. Includes biographical notes, 16-17th c.

Thurstaston

RACKHAM, R.B. 'Notes on the rectors of Thurstaston in the 16th & 17th centuries', *Wirral notes and queries* 2, 1892-3, 68-79.

Wallasey

'Wallasey church in 1634', *Wirral notes and queries* 2, 1893, 16-18. Seat plan.

Wirral Deanery

'Wirral Deanery, 1554', *Wirral notes and queries* 2, 1893, 59, & 67. For 1592, see 52-3 & 54-5; for 1598, see 80-81 & 82; for 1605, see 64-6. Gives names of clergy etc. at visitations.

'The incumbents of the parishes in the Deanery of Wirral, 1618', *C.Sf.* 3rd series 6, 1907, 71. List.

'Report on the Deanery of Wirral about the year 1915', *C.Sf.* 1907, 74 76. Names incumbents and schoolmasters.

Woodchurch

'The rectors of Woodchurch in the Hundred of Wirral and County of Chester, 1588 to 1919', *Genealogist* N.S., 35, 1919, 193-203. Includes pedigrees of Adams, Burches, King and Robin.

B. *Nonconformists.*

For a general introduction to Cheshire nonconformist history, see:

URWICK, WILLIAM,, ed. *Historical sketches of nonconformity in the County Palatine of Chester.* London: Kent & Co., Manchester: Septimus Fletcher, 1864. Topographical survey, listing clergy, *etc.* Detailed.

A brief introduction to sources is provided by:

'Some sources for non-conformist history in Cheshire', *Cheshire history newsletter* 7, 1974, 31-4.

A few brief general notes provide potentially useful information:

'Early nonconformity in Cheshire', *C.Sf.* 3rd series 7, 1910, 3-4. See also 6. Lists grantees of licences for meeting houses.

B., J. 'Religious differences in Cheshire in 1663', *C.Sf.* 3rd series 22, 1927, 60, 61-2, & 63. Lists recusants, Quakers, Anabaptists, and 'Fanatics'.

W., W. 'Recusants and nonconformists, 1669', *C.Sf.* 3rd series 58, 1965, 10-24, *passim.* Presentments made at the Bishop's visitation of the Archdeaconry of Chester.

B[ENNETT], J.H.E. 'Certificates of private houses in Chester for use for religious worship', *C.Sf.* 3rd series 14, 1919, 6. Lists certificates, 1694-6.

Baptists

SELLERS, IAN, ed. *Our heritage: the Baptists of Yorkshire, Lancashire and Cheshire, 1647-1787-1887-1987.* Leech: Yorkshire Baptist Association, 1987.

R., M.H. 'Anabaptists in Shropshire and Cheshire in the eighteenth century', *C.Sf.* 4th series 1, 1966, 2, 4, & 5-66. Includes list of members, 1706, of a church at Stoke on Tern, Shropshire, including Cheshire names.

Congregationalists

MAYOR, S.H. *Cheshire Congregationalism: a brief history.* Chester: W.H. Evans Sons & Co., 1956. Includes list of office holders of the Cheshire Congregational Union, 1806-1956.

POWICKE, FRED. JAMES. *A history of the Cheshire County Union of Congregational churches.* Manchester: Thomas Griffiths & Co., 1907. Includes detailed historical 'account of churches and stations in the Union',

EVANS, GEORGE EYRE. *Record of the Provincial Assembly of Lancashire and Cheshire.* Manchester: H. Rawson and Co., 1896. Biographies of Congregational ministers.

GORDON, A., ed. *Cheshire classis: minutes, 1691-1745.* Chiswick Press, 1919. Includes the names of many Congregational and Presbyterian ministers, *etc.*

Chester

A., C. 'Records of the Matthew Henry Chapel', *C.Sf.* 3rd series 57, 1964, 24-5. In Chester; lists of records, 17-20th c.

Crewe

LITTON, P.M. 'Transfer of members to and from Hightown Congregational Church, Crewe', *N.C.F.H.* 5,(1), 1978, 19. List of transferees, 1895-1902.

Dukinfield

Dukinfield Old Chapel Sunday School: centenary souvenir, 1900. Ashton-under-Lyme: William Brown & Son, 1901. Includes extensive list of persons present at the re-union party.

GORDON, ALEXANDER. *Historical account of Dukinfield Chapel and its school.* Manchester: Cartwright and Rattray, 1896. Includes list of contribution to building fund, 1890, lists of ministers and officers, *etc.,* and many other names.

Stockport

'Church book &c., or, an account of the church of Christ assembling at the chapel in Church-Gate, Stockport', *N.C.F.H.* 9(2), 1982, 62-4.

Methodists

ROSE, E.A. 'Methodism in Cheshire to 1800', *L.C.A.S.* 78, 1975, 22-37. Includes list of chapels, *etc.,* 1801.

SIMPSON, EILEEN. 'Methodist records (not) in the Cheshire Record Office', *Journal of the Lancashire and Cheshire Branch of the Wesley Historical Society* 47(3), 1981, 50-54; 4(4), 1981, 62-5; 4(5), 1982, 90. General discussion of records deposited (or not)

JACKSON, MICHAEL. 'The Wesleyan Methodist historic roll', *Cheshire history* 14, 1984, 27-8. Discussion of the list of contributors to the fund for building Westminster Central Hall; includes list of Lymm contributors, 1898-1908.

'The Wesleyan historic roll', *N.C.F.H.* 10(2), 1953, 36-8.

'Extracts from the Manchester Circuit account book 1752-1762', *Journal of the Lancashire and Cheshire branch of the Wesley Historical Society* 2(4) 1971, 75-7; 2(5), 1972, 89-90; 2(6), 1972, 111-4; 2(7), 129. Lists societies and stewards. The circuit extended to Chester.

Eagle Brow

JACKSON, MICHAEL. 'Eagle Brow Methodist Chapel membership, 1840-1848', *Q.J.L.D.* 2(3), 1979, 10. List.

Lymm

JACKSON, MICHAEL. 'Lymm Primitive Methodist circuit plan, 1874', *J.L.D.H.S.* 1(1), 1985, 5-8. Lists many circuit officers.

Marple

ROSE, E.A. 'Sources for the history of Methodism in Marple and district', *Journal of the Lancashire and Cheshire branch of the Wesley Historical Society* 3(3), 1976, 52-3.

Moravians

'List of ministers who served the Dukinfield Moravians', *Manchester genealogist* 19(1), 1982, 11.

Presbyterians

'Licences to Presbyterian preachers in 1672', *C.Sf.* 3rd series 6, 1907, 68-9. List.
See also Congregationalists

Quakers

'The list of Quakers in Lancashire and Cheshire, c.1670', *Manchester genealogist* 24(3), 1988, 164-5.

'Quakers in Cheshire', *F.H.S.C.J.* 2(4), 1971, 4. Brief note on records.

B., S. 'Quakers in Chester 1653-1656', *C.Sf.* 4th series 5, 1970, 9-28. Account of 'sufferings', mentioning many names.

SANDERS, F. 'The Quakers in Chester under the Protectorate', *J.C.A.H.S.* N.S., 14, 1907, 29-84. Reprints 17th c. tract, giving many names of Quaker 'sufferers'.

TAYLOR, BETTY. 'The decline of Quakers in Cheshire', *N.C.F.H.* 17(3), 1990, 91-6. Includes list of Quakers, 1898.

Roman Catholics.

WARK, K.R. *Elizabethan recusancy in Cheshire.* Cm.S., 3rd series 19, 1971. Includes list of recusants, i.e. Roman Catholics, with biographical notes.

'Cheshire recusants', *C.Sf.* 3rd series 11, 1915, 39. List, 1592.

B., J. 'Cheshire recusants', *C.Sf.* 3rd series 18, 1923, 83-98, *passim.* List, 1610.

MITCHINSON, ALLAN JOSEPH, ed. *The return of the Papists for the Diocese of Chester, 1705.* Wigan: North West Catholic History Society, 1986.

'Roman Catholics in Cheshire in 1706', *C.Sf.* 3rd series 27, 1934, 73-7, *passim.* List.

S., E. 'Return of Papists, 1706', *C.Sf.* 4th series 5, 1970, 32-42. For Cheshire.

WORRAL, E.S., ed. *Return of papists, 1767:*
Diocese of Chester. Occasional publications
1. Catholic Record Society, 1980. Includes
Cheshire, Lancashire, Westmorland and part
of Yorkshire.

Broxton Hundred

B., J. 'Recusants in Broxton Hundred, 1642',
C.Sf. 3rd series **19**, 1924, 51. List from the
subsidy return.

Chester

STURMAN, MARY WINEFRIDE. *Catholicism in
Chester: a double centenary: St. Werburgh's
and St. Francis's, 1875-1975.* Chester: St.
Werburghs Catholic Church, 1975. Includes
lists of priests.
STURMAN, M. WINEFRIDE. 'Catholicism in
Chester: some Catholic families in the
nineteenth century', *Catholic ancestor* **3**(5),
1991, 179-88.

13. EDUCATION

Educational records provide much information
of genealogical interest. A number of general
works on the history of Cheshire education
provide useful information:

C., M., & R., C.D. 'Schoolmasters in Elizabethan
Cheshire', *C.Sf.* 4th series **4**, 1969, 2-6. List,
1563-79, from ecclesiastial records.
ROBSON, DEREK. *Some aspects of education in
Cheshire in the eighteenth century.* Cm.S.,
3rd series **13**. 1966. Includes lists of schools,
schoolmasters, schoolmasters' wills, and
Cheshire boys at Oxford and Cambridge
universities.
ROBSON, D. 'Cheshire education in the 18th
century', *Cheshire round* **1**(5), 1966, 141-6.
Brief general survey.
WALLIS, P.J. 'A preliminary register of old
schools in Lancashire and Cheshire', *H.S.L.C.*
120, 1969, 1-21.

Histories of particular schools may also be
useful. The list which follows is not intended
to be comprehensive; rather, it aims to identify
works which have particular value to
genealogists, providing names of teachers and
students, or other helpful information.

Acton

B[ENNETT], J.H.E. 'Acton Grammar School',
C.Sf. 3rd series **47**, 1953, 57-63, *passim.* Lists
original feoffees, 1662, and others
subsequently connected with the governance
of the school.
See also Nantwich

Altrincham

DORE, R.N. *The history of Altrincham
Grammar School for Boys 1912-62.*
Altrincham: Mackie and Co., [1962.] Includes
various school lists.

Audlem

REDWOOD, BRIAN C. 'Audlem Free Grammar
School', *J.C.A.H.S.* **51**, 1964, 31-53. Includes
notes on headmasters, 17-19th c.

Barthomley

'Barthomley School', *C.Sf.* 3rd series **48**, 1956,
22-9. Lists some pupils, 17th c., with
biographical notes.

Caldy

BROWN, CHARLES D. *Deeds and documents concerning the school founded by William Glegg, esq., of Calday Grange, in the year 1636, with notes, remarks and explanations thereon.* Liverpool: T. Brakell, 1890. Includes abstracts of 16 deeds, also notes on masters, *etc.*

PROTHEROE, M.J. *A history of Calday Grange Grammar School, West Kirby, 1636-1976.* [West Kirby]: The School, *et al,* 1976. General study; includes list of sources.

Cheadle Hulme

BAKER, G.J.M. *A history of Cheadle Hulme School (The Manchester Warehousemen & Clerks' Orphan Schools) 1855-1955.* Manchester: Manchester Warehousemen and Clerks Orphan Schools, 1955. Includes rolls of honour, 1914-18 and 1939-45.

Chester

KENNETT, ANNETTE M. *Chester schools: a guide to the school archives, with a brief history of education in the city from 1539 to 1972.* Chester: City Record Office, 1973.

PHILIPS, GLADYS. *A short history of the Queens School, Chester, 1878-1978.* Chester: the School, 1978. General history; many names mentioned.

Frodsham

RINGROSE, F.D. 'Frodsham Grammar School', *C.Sf.* 3rd series 1, 1896, 88-90. Includes list of masters, etc., 17-18th c.

Hazel Grove

'Have you lost some children?', *N.C.F.H.* 10(2), 1983, 52-3. 1841 census for boarding schools in Hazel Grove and Hollingworth.

Hollingworth

See Hazel Grove

Lymm

KAY, DERRICK M. *The history of Lymm Grammar School.* Altrincham: John Sherratt & Son 1960. Includes list of headmasters, 1592-1934, and a bibliography, *etc.*

Macclesfield

WILMOT, DARWIN. *A short history of the Grammar School, Macclesfield, 1503 to 1910, with lists of masters, exhibitioners, copy of the admission register, of Sir John Percyvale's will, and of the charter of King Edward VI.* Macclesfield: Claye, Brown & Claye, 1910. The register covers 1775-1909.

Marple

SWINDELLS, GLADYS A. *History of education in Marple, 1603-1971.* [Chester]: Cheshire County Council, Libraries and Museums; [Marple]: Marple Antiquarian Society, 1974. General study.

Nantwich

LLOYD. EDWARD. *Nantwich and Acton Grammar School, 1560-1960.* Nantwich: F.G. Morris, 1960. Includes list of headmasters, 1623-1951.

Northwich

COX, MARJORIE. *A history of Sir John Deane's Grammar School, Northwich, 1557-1908.* Manchester: Manchester University Press, 1975. Extensive; includes list of masters, notes on school records, detailed bibliographical notes, *etc.*

Stockport

G., W.H. 'Headmasters of Stockport Grammar School, *A.N.Q.* 4, 1884, 88. List, 1609-1847.

VARLEY, BENJAMIN. *The history of Stockport Grammar School, including the life of Sir Edmond Shaa, Kt., P.C., founder.* 3rd ed. Manchester: Manchester University Press, 1957. Includes Shaa family pedigrees, 14-16th c., rent roll 1496-7, list of early Stopfordians at Cambridge, list of masters, *etc.*

WILD, W.I. *The history of the Stockport Sunday School and its branch schools, together with a record of all movements connected with the Stockport Sunday School.* The author, 1891. Includes various lists of officers, committee, visitors, teachers, *etc.,* 1784-1891.

Wallasey

EGGLESHAW, MAURICE. *The history of Wallasey Grammar School.* Wallasey: M.Eggleshaw, 1970. Includes list of head boys, 1877-1969, notes on the Meoles family, *etc.*

Wilmslow

POLLARD, M. 'Wilmslow National School, 8 November 1830', *N.C.F.H.* **16**(2), 1989, 39. List of pupils embroidered on a sampler.

Witton

'Witton (or Northwich) Grammar School', *C.Sf.* 3rd series **3**, 1901, 73-4, 76-7 & 80-81. Calendar of deeds, 18th c.

Out of County

ASHDOWN, ELAINE I. '1881 census return for Llysfaen, nr. Colwyn Bay, North Wales: list of scholars in boy's school, Tanllwyfan, including Cheshire boys', *N.C.F.H.* **18**(2), 1988, 31-2.

Universities

AXON, ERNEST. 'Lancashire and Cheshire admissions to Gonville and Caius College, Cambridge, 1558 to 1678', *L.C.A.S.* **6**, 1888, 74-97.

'Admissions at Emanuel College, Cambridge, 1610-1723', *P.N.* **4**, 1884, 78-81. Lists for Cheshire and Lancashire.

GRIGSON, FRANCIS. 'Admissions to Jesus College, Cambridge, 1618-1719', *P.N.* **3**, 1883, 266-8. List for Cheshire and Lancashire.

'Admissions to St. Johns College, Cambridge', *C.Sf.* 3rd series **2**, 1896, 111-12 & 114-5, 132-4 & 135-7. See also 142. From Cheshire, 1629-1715.

'Cheshire schools and masters', *C.Sf.* 3rd series **5**, 1904, 116. List, 1715-57, from R.F. Scott's *Admissions to St. Johns College, Cambridge.*

'Admissions to St. Johns College, Cambridge, 1715-1767', *C.Sf.* 3rd series, **6**, 1907, 25, 27-8 & 29-30.

CANTAB. 'Brasenose College, Oxford, and Cheshire', *C.Sf.* 3rd series **29**, 1935, 18-27, *passim.* Lists Cheshire students *etc.*

14. MIGRATION

Many Cheshire people have migrated to foreign parts over the centuries. There is a useful listing of emigrants to America, and a number of brief notes which may just contain the name you are looking for.

COLDHAM, PETER WILSON. *Bonded passengers to America volume VIII: Northern Circuit 1665-1775.* Baltimore: Genealogical Publishing, 1983.

TAYLOR, BETTY. 'Liverpool lists of emigrants', *N.C.F.H.* **18**(1), 1991, 30-31. List of servants who sailed to Virginia on the *Liberty,* 1698, from Liverpool Corporation records. Includes several Cheshire names.

LITTON, P., & McKENNA, S. 'A list of Cheshire residents sentenced to transportation, January 1828 to October, 1829', *N.C.F.H.* **6**(2), 1979, 42-3. From Quarter Session records. Not all were necessarily transported.

'[List of transportees from Chester Castle, 1829]', *N.C.F.H.* **15**(2), 1988, 39.

Family Name Index

Adams 25, 86
Aldersey 46, 68
Alsager 41
Angier 31
Anglezer 46
Anglizer 46
Antrobus 72
Anyon 46
Arderne 46

Bache 24
Baggalegh 41
Baguley 47
Bailey 47
Ball 47
Banbury 35
Barker 41
Barnston 47, 72
Barret 47
Barrington 47
Barrow 47
Bars 47
Bateson 24
Batha 47
Bathoe 47
Bebington 57
Becket 41
Bennett 41
Betson 47
Beverley 47
Bird 47
Blackburne 47
Bold 47
Booth 14, 24
Bostock 47
Bostoke 47
Bosyer 48
Bowdon 19
Boydell 41
Bramfield 42
Bramhall 49
Brereton 13, 48, 72
Brerewood 48
Bridge 24
Bridges 48
Brock 22, 48
Brooke 48

Broster 16, 25, 36
Broughton 48, 79
Bruerton 48
Bryson 48
Bulkeley 42, 48, 74
Bunbury 40, 48
Burches 86
Burgancy 42
Burges 48
Burnham 75
Byram 69

Calveley 42, 48
Cambourne 23
Candland 48
Carden 72
Caveley 48
Chalyner 48
Chamber 48, 54
Chantrell 48
Cholmondeley 72
Cholmondley 59
Clutton 49
Clyff 49
Coker 49
Cooke 49
Corbet 43
Corles 42
Cotes 42
Cotgrave 49
Cottingham 42, 70
Cotton 24
Coventry 49
Cragg 42
Crawfurd 14
Crookhall 49
Croughton 49
Crymes 49

Danyers 74
Daryngton 49
Davenport 49
Davie 49
Davies 49
Davye 49
Dayne 49
De La Pole 57

De Tabley 23
Denson 49
Derbishire 49
Derby, Earls of 71
Deykyn 49
Dod 49
Dodyngton 49
Domville 73
Doncaster 68
Drihurst 54
Drinkwater 50
Duncalf 50
Dunfont 73

Egerton 23, 42, 50, 72
Egerton-Warburton 72
Elcock 50
Englefield 50
Erneys 69

Fernehed 50
Fitton 42, 50, 74
Fletcher 50, 53
Fownes 24
Francis 50
Frodsham 42
Fyton 50
Fytton 50

Gardner 36, 50
Garratt 35
Gerrard 74
Gill 50
Glasier 50
Gleave 50
Glegg 42, 57, 71, 89
Goodacre 50
Goodicar 50
Goose 51
Goostrey 85
Gravener 51
Gravenor 51
Greene 51
Grey 72
Griffin 51
Griffith 51
Grosvenor 51

Place Name Index

Bedfordshire 76

Berkshire 76

Buckinghamshire 76
Bledlow 62

Caernarvonshire
Llandegai 42

Cambridgeshire
Cambridge 89, 90
Cambridge; Gonville & Caius College 91
Cambridge; Emmanuel College 91
Cambridge; Jesus College 91
Cambridge; Saint Johns College 91

Cheshire
Acton 35, 85, 89, 90
Acton Grange 62, 63
Adlington 79
Agden 48
Alderley 29, 35, 57, 65
Alderley Edge 65
Aldford 51, 52, 68
Alpraham 12
Alsager 65
Altrincham 10, 16, 63, 65, 66, 79, 89
Alvanley 57
Antrobus 35
Appleton 12, 29
Appleton Thorn 35
Arley Hall 73
Ashley 13, 54, 65
Ashton 49, 55, 57
Ashton upon Mersey 10, 26, 35, 60, 85
Astbury 35
Aston 12, 42, 85
Aston by Budworth 59
Aston by Sutton 42, 62, 63
Aston Grange 62, 63
Aston Hall 69
Aston on Mersey 23
Audlem 35, 89
Bache 73
Backford 40
Baddiley 35
Badington 51
Baguley 10, 65

Baguley Hall 41
Balterley 57
Barnston 35, 49
Barnton 35, 61, 62
Barrow 12, 79, 85
Bartherton 51
Barthomley 36, 50, 86, 89
Barton 62
Bebington 29, 36, 55, 58, 68
Beeston 54
Bertles 56
Bickley 68
Bidston 29, 36, 41, 57, 85
Birkenhead 16, 30, 65, 69
Birkenhead Priory 68
Blacon 69
Bollington 36, 41, 65
Bosley 30, 36
Boughton 14, 63
Bowdon 10, 30, 43, 52, 65
Bradwall 56
Bramhall 30, 65, 69
Bramhall Hall 36, 61, 74
Bredbury 13
Brereton 41
Bridge Trafford 56
Brimstage 69, 74
Bromborough 30, 36, 50, 57, 60
Bromhall 51
Brooklands 65
Broxton 59, 60
Broxton Hundred 59, 66, 89
Bruera 30
Bruern Stapleford 11, 47
Bucklow 66
Bucklow Hundred 12, 59
Bunbury 12, 36, 42, 52, 56, 79
Burland 79
Burton 19, 30, 46, 50, 61, 62, 69
Caldy 62, 69, 90
Capenhurst 36
Capesthorne 30
Carden 73
Castle Northwich 12
Cheadle 16
Cheadle Bulkeley 79
Cheadle Hulme 36, 90

Author Name Index

A., C. 87
A., F. 47-57, 68, 83
Addleshaw, G. 21
Addy, J. 11, 14
Adman, P. 11
Alexander, J. 77
Allan, A. 14
Alldridge, N. 12
Anderson, A. 30
Angus-Butterworth, A. 35
Antrobus, R. 59
Appleby, J. 37
Arber, E. 80
Armstrong, J. 23
Ashdown, E. 91
Ashmore, O. 9
Atkinson, J. 34
Awty, B. 24
Axon, E. 84, 85, 91
Axon, G. 32
Aylett, P. 21

B., J. 52, 67-69, 72, 78, 87-89
B., R. 72
B., S. 88
B., W. 79
Bagshaw, S. 64
Baker, G. 90
Ball, T. 23
Balshaw, C. 65
Barber, E. 30, 80
Barker, E. 74
Barlow, T. 9
Barnes, P. 78
Barraclough, G. 68, 77, 78
Baskerville, S. 11
Bayliss, A. 30
Beamont, W. 12, 70, 73, 75
Beaver, C. 44
Beazley, E. 15
Beazley, F. 18, 28, 30, 34,
   36, 37, 39-42, 46-57, 60, 70
Bebbington, C. 33
Beck, J. 10
Bennett, J. 15, 21, 30, 33, 36,
   37, 39-43, 47, 49-57, 68-70,
   76, 78, 80, 82, 85-87, 89

Bennett, M. 10, 84
Beresford, J. 80
Bethell, D. 39
Bingham, P. 37
Birch, W. 68
Black, W. 77
Blackwell, S. 28
Blair, C. 35, 42
Blinkhorn, M. 11
Booth, J. 72
Booth, P. 10, 58, 71, 76-78
Bostock, A. 25
Bostock, R. 22
Boulton, H. 80
Bowland, J. 86
Boyd, A. 81, 83
Bratt, C. 17, 37
Bridge, J. 24
Bridgeman, G. 84
Brigg, T. 36
Brooks, L. 24
Broster, P. 64
Brown, C. 90
Brown, W. 66
Brownbill, J. 68, 84
Buchan, G. 61
Bulkeley, E. 33
Bullock, C. 86
Bullock, M. 37-39
Bullough, H. 36
Bulmer, J. 28
Burdett, P. 66
Burne, R. 11, 80, 85
Burnley, R. 24
Burt, R. 24
Burton, A. 24
Burtt, J. 56

C., E. 55, 76
C., M. 80, 89
Calladine, A. 24
Calvert, A. 25
Cantab 91
Capener, J. 62, 63
Carr, A. 76
Carr, P. 30, 32
Cartlidge, J. 13

Chadwick, P. 17, 83
Challinor, P. 11
Challinor, R. 24
Chaloner, W. 12
Cheetham, F. 82
Chester City Record Office
   15
Choice, J. 31, 33
Choice, L. 29-33
Chorley, B. 50, 63
Christopher, M. 35
Church, C. 32, 82
Churton, W. 26
Clark, P. 11
Clarke, A. 36, 38, 39, 41
Clarke, J. 22
Clarke, R. 41
Clarke, W. 37, 82
Claye, W. 25
Clayton, D. 15, 68, 77, 78
Clayton, G. 43
Clemesha, H. 69
Clopper, L. 79
Cockburn, J. 10
Coldham, P. 91
Commonwealth War Graves
   Commission 26
Connah, G. 86
Cooke, J. 14, 26
Corry, J. 65
Cowdroy, W. 64
Cowley, R. 20
Cox, M. 90
Craig, J. 28
Craig, R. 25
Crampton, J. 82
Crawfurd, G. 14
Crofton, H. 24
Crookenden, A. 26, 27
Crosby, A. 19
Crossley, F. 22, 35, 48
Croston, J. 41
Crump, J. 30
Cullen, M. 46, 69
Curry, A. 71
Curtis, A. 28
Curtis, T. 10